THE
FAMILY
BUSINESS

THE
FAMILY
BUSINESS

Adrian Kenny

THE LILLIPUT PRESS
DUBLIN

First published 1999 by
THE LILLIPUT PRESS LTD
62–63 Sitric Road, Arbour Hill, Dublin 7,
Ireland.

A CIP record for this title is available from
the British Library.

ISBN 1 901866 37 8

*The Lilliput Press receives financial assistance from
An Chomhairle Ealaíon / The Arts Council of Ireland.*

Set in 11 on 14 Bembo by Sheila Stephenson

Printed in Ireland by
ColourBooks of Baldoyle, Dublin

To Ruth
again

THE
FAMILY
BUSINESS

The phone rang. It was Kevin, my younger brother. I tensed a little.

'Are you sitting down?'

'Why?'

He spoke in the calm voice our father had perfected, losing or casting off control as he came to the point. 'I'm selling the business.'

I sat down. 'Oh.'

'Yes, I've been thinking about it for a while now. I think it's right for me to make the move at this stage. We're going to live in Scotland.'

I risked a jab—we were barely on speaking terms anyway: 'Celia must like that.'

'Yes, we're looking forward to it, now that we've taken the plunge.' Our father's calm voice again. 'Look, I'll be talking to you. I want to ring the others.'

'OK.'

Click.

★

Celia rang next morning. 'You heard? Well, what do you think?' Her bright Scots voice sent a shiver of anger through me.

'I've been expecting it for years.'

She laughed, skating around unpleasantness. 'Everybody thinks it's my idea, but—'

'Of course.' I cut her short.

Silence. Then: 'It's just for two years initially, while I study for the ministry.'

'The good old Kirk.'

Simmer simmer. Then—'The trouble with you, Adrian, is that you think there's no other religion in the world except Roman Catholicism.'

'No, Celia.' Angry now, so angry I was falling into the family trick, into our father's cool calm slow voice. 'Most of the time I can't stand the Catholic Church, or the Anglican, or the Jewish or the Moslem. I just think Scots Presbyterianism is the dregs of the lot.'

'We must have a chat about this—'

'Let's!'

'—before we leave.' She sounded as if she was smiling. I banged down the phone.

Mama: 'Oh wait till the city of Dublin hears that Kennys is for sale …'

27 MARCH

First advertisements in the newspapers. 'For sale as a going concern. The long-established retail footwear and sports business of Kennys Ltd. Branches at …'

Family row. It seems that Noel went out to Stillorgan when Kevin wasn't there and helped himself to half a dozen pairs of shoes. Kevin called and devoured him.

And now Noel is organizing a family farewell dinner, ordering a cake iced with 'SCOTLAND HERE WE COME!'

I said I wouldn't go.

Noel: 'You miserable git.'

Incredible.

But Noel has always wanted above everything else to avoid trouble.

Mama asked me to visit Kevin and say goodbye.

He answered the door. Bow tie, horn-rimmed reading-glasses, French-looking russet herringbone suit. I thought: Celia's doing. I said: 'I dropped in to say goodbye.'

'Come in.' Boyish brotherly smile from Kevin. Is that the outside only? Or the inside too? I followed him down the big empty echoing hall. 'Most of the furniture has gone ahead. We're camping downstairs.'

Down in the kitchen Celia and the children were sitting about. The housekeeper—still there—was clearing the table. Celia smiled up from coffee and the English *Times*. Kevin went over to the ironing-board and said, 'I'll just finish this, then I'll get you a drink'—and resumed ironing a shirt. I thought: you earn the money, you pay the housekeeper—and you iron your shirt. But that was always Celia's attraction for him: the less she was like Mama, the more he liked her. Celia put down *The Times*.

'That awful paper,' I said—and even that made my legs shake.

'Why?' Celia smiled. When I didn't reply she turned to the housekeeper—'Jenny, have you met Adrian? Kevin's brother.'

Big smile from Jenny. Answering smile from me, my forehead wrinkling in pretend confusion. 'Are you Celia's sister?'

Nice one, but my knees were knocking now. Kevin looked up laughing from the ironing-board, looked quickly down again as Celia's forehead clouded. It cleared again. 'We never really got to know each other, did we?'

'Not really.' Thanks be to God. I looked at the children lying in *Homes and Gardens* arrangement on the kitchen floor. Matthew in Viyella shirt with Dinky cars. Joanne, knees tucked up in long gingham dress, reading *Adrian Mole*. Heather lying on stomach reading a teen magazine, bare legs pedalling the air.

'Hi,' I said.

'Scotch?' Kevin poured big glassfuls, gave one to Celia, one to me, poured a smaller one for himself.

'Here's to the big trip.' I raised my glass.

'I can't wait.' Celia said.

I spoke slowly to keep my voice from trembling. 'I never really liked the Scots.'

'Oh.' Celia's voice sounded as if it was being held in rein. 'Have you met many?'

One too many. 'Just a few.'

A brotherly smile from Kevin. Then, in a husbandly voice: 'Why's that?'

'They're so …' fucking canny, and they never did a damn thing this past two hundred years but act as England's butler '… careful.'

Joanne looked up from *Adrian Mole*. 'I don't agree.'

'You don't?' I did an old uncle's smile, to hide my timidity, and I thought suddenly—that's why Kevin married Celia: to get away from this awful family timidity. She had the whip-hand now, nodding encouragement as Joanne went on—'I don't think you can make generalizations like that about countries.'

'Perhaps not.' I did my avuncular smile again, as Celia reached out and slapped a high five on Joanne's raised hand, then turned to smile at me.

Fuck you, the smile said. I've had to be polite to you these past twenty years, to read your crappy books, put up with your mother, your sniping, your Church, your banana republic. Not any more, baby. Fuck you.

I finished my drink. 'Well—' I stood up, yawned casually. Well, Celia, you won. It was a long dirty fight but fair dues to you, you won. Your husband's had a vasectomy, he's sold the family business, the cash is in the bank, you're all off to the UK. The man who made the cash, an Irish Catholic Republican peasant, is dead and his widow is dying. 'I'd better be going,' I said.

Kevin walked up the stairs with me to the door, clapped me gently on the shoulder in sympathy, had shut the door before I reached the front gate. Around the corner, out of sight, I wept—of course. Jesus Mary and Joseph those West of Ireland tears.

30 JUNE

Kevin & Co. left Ireland. I went out to my agent, handed over my manuscript. On the way home I passed by Palmerston Park. Bins outside Kevin's house overturned by treasure-hunters. An Alex uniform, an electric iron, an atlas littered across the path. I took the atlas.

Called to Mama to cheer her up. Maddening as ever. A fussing, nerve-racking old woman. I go to the toilet and she calls, 'Where is he? A-drian! Where are you?'

Kevin was right to leave. He had to leave. He wanted to leave. And without Celia he could never have done it.

Last impression of Celia: the cat who swallowed the canary.

Last impression of Kevin: worn, lean, eyes hooded.

It's just struck me: I handed over the manuscript of my autobiography on the very day Kevin left. That was no coincidence. I had a hand, we all had a hand in smashing up the family business. Think about that, Mr Detached Artist.

Where will I begin?

Begin when you began to grow up, when you left that hidey-hole in the country.

THE BRAZEN HEAD

— I —

I shut the door and turned the key—as long as my hand and five times older—and put it in my pocket, felt a piece of chalk there and threw it away. A teacher no more. I looked in the window to see that the fire was alright, and felt even more lonely. My last bits of rubbish were making a blaze, throwing light across the bare floor.

A back avenue of old beech trees closed over, a green tunnel echoing with wood-pigeon calls—that was what I'd pictured when I wrote to the landowner asking for a lease of this gate-lodge. The timber merchant must have received a similar business-like agreement. Now there was only a scar of mud curving up the hillside; all the trees gone except a spindly few behind the lodge, which I'd bought for five pounds.

They were still my trees, I thought, four beech and a larch. I pulled the big gate shut, latched it to its comrade, got into my car and drove away.

10 JULY 1972. Moved into the Brazen Head ... My room was two floors up, at the back. Halfway down the corridor was a brass tap, a tin basin underneath, in it a cocktail

sausage of cat shit. I was so sweaty from carrying up bags, books, typewriter that I turned the tap on anyhow, caught a handful of water and splashed my face. Then I went into my room, shut the door and lay on the bed.

Through a dusty window I could see the shape of Power's distillery and behind it an evening sun. On one of the buildings, square and flat-roofed, there was a meadow. A man was mowing it with a scythe, a kestrel hung over his head, a breeze rippled the grass.

The room was small, very warm, the window sealed with newspaper and the fireplace too. The floor sloped like a school desk. As I looked at the sun sink behind the meadow, I wondered if this had been my father's room. He had lived here in the thirties when he first came to Dublin, which was how I had come to hear of this place. The sun vanished, the man put the scythe on his shoulder and walked off the skyline and I fell asleep.

A radio woke me and I lay in the dark listening to a BBC voice across the corridor. The cat shit had gone from the basin but when I went into the bathroom I saw it floating in the toilet bowl. I added my own and pulled the chain. From the window I could see down into the front yard where Mrs Cooney the landlady stood smoking a cigarette, gazing up a whitewashed alley to the street. The passing traffic shook the bathroom window and floor. It excited me: my own city seemed as new-strange as it must have to my father forty years before. Mrs Cooney dropped her cigarette end, ground it thoughtfully under her heel and went back into the bar. I washed my hands and went downstairs.

The corridor sloped too, and the stairs, the ceiling. A greasy dusty feel to everything. A big patched landing window was covered with scratches, probably by people trying to match the copperplate writing cut in one pane—'John Lonergan Waterford halted here the 7th August 1700.' A grandfather clock ticked so slowly it seemed about to stop. I went into the bar.

A few men, each in his own melancholy island of space, were passing a letter around. A tall man with a long flushed face, a long bitter mouth, was last to read it. He sneered and shoved it back across the counter to Mrs Cooney, who shoved it out again towards me, saying, 'What do you make of that?'

The man who had sneered turned slowly on his high stool as if he had a crick in his neck; sneered at me then raised a glass of whiskey to thin lips. I looked at the letter:

Hi!

We at *Life* are presently compiling a Great Bars of the World series. We would appreciate a short history of your bar plus any interesting legends associated with it (ghosts, personalities, etc.). A recipe for the house speciality—cocktails, whiskey mixes—would be appreciated.

Yours sincerely, Gail Lotrop.

A man in the corner spoke—a thin Cavan accent—'I wouldn't tell them anything.'

'What's the softest part of a Cavan man?' the bitter-faced man said—a low West of Ireland voice. 'The teeth,' he said and when Mrs Cooney laughed he fell into a small frenzy of embarrassment or excitement, rubbing big red hands together, uncrossing his legs and twining them about the barstool legs, shifting the tilt of his hat. He emptied his glass and pushed it forward an inch. While Mrs Cooney poured another measure, he lit a cigarette and inhaled deeply. I waited for the smoke to appear.

'What's *Life* at all?'—another voice, a Donegal accent. A big elderly man, bald red head grazing the lampshade, pitted swollen nose the same colour as the lemonade he drank.

'A magazine,' the man sitting next to me said. Dublin.

'Is that so?' Touchy.

'It is so.'

Mrs Cooney shoved the letter amongst withered dockets behind the till, poured herself a drink and came out from behind the bar. 'Well, Michael.' She sat down beside the Cavan man. The bitter man swallowed his drink and went out.

'Goodnight, Dick,' she said after him. He didn't reply. I heard the stairs creak.

'Do you live here?' I turned to the Dublin man.

He shook his head and we chatted. Mrs Cooney was from the North, he said, she liked the Northerners best. Pat was from Donegal, Michael from Cavan. 'But they're all the same. Very ...' he blessed himself a few times contemptuously '... religious. Do you know the last time I was at Mass? Guess.'

'When?'

'When I was twenty-four. How old do you think I am now? Guess.'

'Sixty?'

'Sixty-one.'

The stairs creaked again, more old men appeared, the bar filled. A man with a heavy white moustache stained tobacco-yellow sat down beside us, began to pour his bottle of stout, paused and began to talk—a slow old-fashioned Dublin accent; poured, paused again and went on talking about an increase in his Guinness pension. Mrs Cooney went into the kitchen. A whiff of Irish stew. Already I felt at home, tucked into place, out of sight like that letter among the old dockets.

But wasn't that—I was standing suddenly—what had happened in the gate-lodge I'd just left? My stomach swooned with misery at the memory of those long lonely evenings by the log fire, the nightly walk down to the crossroads pub so like this bar; the ritual cynical exchanges, the varnish of ancient wisdom those country voices gave to the tritest remark, the solitary walk home looking up at the stars, tipsy happiness draining away as I entered my empty cottage.

'I'm going out.' I put my head into the kitchen. 'What time do you lock up?'

'I'll give you a key.' Mrs Cooney went on eating, a cigarette smoked in an ashtray by her plate. 'And a key for the gate.' She went to the pot, spooned more potatoes, onions, soup on to the plate. 'What time would you be back?'

'It might be midnight.'

'Och,' opening a drawer, 'that's early.' Gazing in absently, taking out a key. 'That's for the door anyway.' She stirred some knives and spoons about.

I noticed the gate as I went out to the street—a grid of blackened iron slats like a portcullis, looking as if it might have belonged once in the old city wall; guarding now from night attack a tailor's sweatshop throbbing still with sewing-machine and transistor music, Mrs Cooney's white Austin Mini, and the Brazen Head itself. The sign, a face masked anonymous by many yellow skins of paint, gazed down at me as I stood making up my mind where to go.

Up the hill by the old wall would take me south, out to Rathmines—home, where my father, my mother would be sitting now, watching TV. No thanks. Down to the left I could see the Liffey, slicked orange by quay lights, swollen by a full tide, reflecting in shattered pieces the Four Courts' serene façade. Wide smoky clouds drifted east over the city, revealing, concealing stars. Yes, and yes again.

Stephen—short, broad-chested, handsome-faced—was sitting alone with a pint, smoking a very thin roll-up, reading *Rolling Stone*. He glanced up as I entered. A long white silk scarf and a schoolgirl's grey gabardine hung open about him, reserving space on either side. I sat on a stool by the marble-top table and he settled more easily into the red leatherette.

'So,' he raised a hand, caught the barman's eye and passed on my order like an interpreter, 'what are you doing abroad at this hour of night?'

This was more than I had hoped for—alone with Stephen, my only contact with literary Dublin. I was twenty-five, the double doors of family and school/college friends seemed about to slide apart, revealing the World. So far they had opened about an inch, a crack giving a glimpse of electric freedom, threatening to close again at any moment—like Peter's door when I had called on him.

I had told Stephen about Peter at our last meeting but it had gone down so well I thought I could risk repeating it. Had to, because now my pint was arriving, Stephen paying for it as naturally as if he had ordered it for himself, turning to me with another quizzical smile.

Peter Barrett. I knew him from school—where else?—but vaguely, for he had been ahead of me. In fact I had only a single memory of him there: back from hospital, sitting alone on a bench with a crutch while the rest of us knelt for morning Rosary. Ahead of me at college too, another single memory: Peter, haggard in an old coat, reading his poems to the literary society in a voice of such conviction I knew they must mean something. Vanishing then, reappearing a few years later one Sunday morning as I walked our dog up Palmerston Road: Peter standing gripping two railing spearheads, looking over them at a house; and still there when I came back from my round of the park an hour later. From a newspaper notice came the next scrap of news—Peter and the girl who lived in that house had married in London. Then a magazine he had started there appeared in Dublin shops. To my wonder I had written a story. I sent it to him. A postcard accepting it decided me to give up the teaching job I'd just got and go to London.

('What a foolish young man you are.' Stephen rolled a cigarette for me, pushed it and his matches across the table.)

Up Ladbroke Grove, past the Lord Elgin, under the railway bridge, turn left down Oxford Gardens. I put Peter's postcard in my pocket and rang the bell. The door opened an inch and his long pale face looked out warily.

He lived on the top floor, a surprisingly bright flat after the ratty stairs. TV light spilled out a half-open door. I followed him tiptoe past it into a big tangerine-painted sitting-room.

Books, serious-looking magazines and records standing on end against the skirting-boards. Purple paper poppies in a wine bottle on the mantelpiece. A black typewriter, a smoking cigarette, a bottle of Newcastle Brown on the table.

The TV gunfire in the next room stopped and Niamh came in. I had seen her last in college in her graduation gown. Now she was wearing a blue cotton miniskirt, sharing the bottle of Newcastle as we talked.

Talking, laughing with a poet! I hadn't met one before but there was no denying Peter the title. After light general talk about home, he eased the conversation into gear and we each produced our CV for the past half-dozen years. His was a Catherine Wheel: left home, left college without a degree, entered and left a mental hospital. At first glance mine was similar: third-class degree, left home for America, brilliant nervous breakdown. But Peter's career—as our old English teacher Fr Wilmot would have said—had style. His jobs, for instance. At the moment he was working in Madame Tussaud's Planetarium, 'moving the heavens' as he said with a sigh. Before that—sigh—he had worked for Securicor. Niamh's blue miniskirt had been his uniform shirt. And as well he was editing the magazine which would be publishing my story, which—his voice lowered gravely, reminding me again of Fr Wilmot—he would discuss later.

('You must let me see that,' Stephen put in.

'I wrote to you asking—'

'Did I not reply? How very bad-mannered of me. So …?')

So, over the next few months—I stayed in their flat for the summer—Peter and I discussed my story, Peter's poetry, everything. Everything Peter remembered. ECT in mental hospitals had wiped away part of his memory. All he had been made to learn at school, at home, by compulsion, had gone too. I remembered everything: Troy weight, Young Lochinvar, the length of the Shannon. Peter had forgotten even the second half of the Hail Mary.

[23]

Slipping back into the flat at night from a party or a film or the Lord Elgin, and finding Peter with his head turbaned in his hands, I felt like a healthy slob. When he showed me what he had written while I was out, I couldn't understand it. I nodded, sipped more Newcastle Brown, read it again. Even when Peter took me through it line by line I couldn't see it, but then I had got a headache trying to follow Cyril Connolly's *Enemies of Promise*. Peter sighed and laid the paper by the typewriter.

'Give the writing a try,' my father had said, as he handed me five hundred pounds (for the car he had bought me, which I had sold back to him), 'and if it doesn't work out ... well, I wasn't much of a success when I was your age.' If only he had been like Peter's father, I thought: kicked me out, put me in an asylum. But he wasn't, he hadn't. Maybe that explained what the few other stories I had now written were about? Peter touched gently on their similarity—they all featured a simpleton, male or female, happily trapped in Irish countryside.

'Turning now to 'Bicycles'—and may I say, and I mean this with *absolute* sincerity, that though I entirely see the justification for the detailed description of the bicycle, artistically—if I may use that awful word ... Incidentally, shouldn't it be "Sturmey Archer" in that reference to the three-speed gears?'

'What did I say?'

With hand-wringing courtesy Peter explained that I had written '*Sturmley* Archer'. 'And I think, for once, I can speak with ... authority, having used one at school to speed me on my way ... to those men with wings ... that do not fly ...'

Peter could carry this off because he was so serious, stopping to choose his words, hesitating, apologizing. 'However, since we cannot speak in poetry all the time, my remarks on a story of such ... shining integrity ...'

'You didn't like it?'

'It's very easy to be hard.'

'I was just trying to get across ...' I realized I hadn't an idea what I was trying to get across.

Peter ran a hand through his hair in sympathy. 'You have to cut the umbilical cord, Adrian.'

When he was in the pub with other writers whose names I knew from the spines of books, he was the same, silent sometimes all evening. The Muses' font wasn't just on Mount Helicon but anywhere, everywhere, so all behaviour had to be of fitting gravity. The Queen's portrait on a pound note, the bubbles in the beer it bought were given the same agonized attention Peter gave to his writing.

'"Step out the road, Aunt Kate ..."'

'I don't follow that.' I ran my hand through my hair. 'Who's talking—you?'

'Ignore the line ending,' Peter leaned over my shoulder, 'and go on to the full stop.'

By autumn I didn't need these poetry grinds, and as well as understanding Peter's poems I could understand his friends' poems too. It was like learning a new language. But when a postcard came from the school I had left—they were stuck for a new teacher, would I be interested in coming back?—I gulped at it like fresh air.

As soon as I accepted, I was smothered by guilt. Here was Peter running a hand through his hair—a gesture he had gently but firmly repossessed—urging me to return to Ireland, painting up the horror of London where he was going to remain.

The night before I left we went to the Lord Elgin. I watched him stand behind the ranks of West Indians at the bar, waiting to be served—as if waiting not to be served. New customers arrived either side of him, were noticed, got their beer. Peter stood still, raised his pound note half an inch, let it drop again, maybe an inch and a half. Even his suit—he had been 'working all day under the night sky'—sigh—was like a non-suit: off-the-peg shapeless, crumpled brown trousers falling over black shoes, with a woeful matching brown tie.

'Two pints,' I said and the barman nodded.

'Thanks,' Peter sighed, and I felt like a spiv.

Beside his absolute helplessness I felt unclean—literally. One day after he had taken a bath I went into the bathroom and saw the water he had forgotten to let out—clear as new-run water.

We drank to my return home. Home: Peter rinsed the word about his mouth and swallowed. I reminded him that I wasn't going home, wasn't even going back to live in the school. Old Major Daly had answered my letter asking for a lease of his back gate-lodge. I had noticed it on Sunday crocodile walks with the schoolboys: that cut-stone fairy-tale cottage at the foot of an avenue of ancient beech trees curving up the hillside, echoing with wood-pigeon calls. I kept quiet about that, told Peter about the hardship ahead—no water, no electricity ... Under the table I clenched my hands. I could hardly wait to get back there.

'So what are you doing up here then?'

'I left—'

Stephen glanced away suddenly as the door opened, his face showing much greater interest. 'Helen—'

A young woman came in, swaying, looking about: pale face, long brown hair, wearing a man's overcoat, a small hat with artificial flowers. A breath of expensive perfume as she brushed by me and sat down beside Stephen—he drew his girl's overcoat and the white scarf about him at once.

A vague Hello, an English voice, and she got up again, went to the bar, returned with a pint for me, another for Stephen, then a glass of red wine for herself. She spilled half of it on her coat as she sat unsteadily down again.

'That's my coat, cunty,' he said.

'Then here's some money for you, fuck-face.' She shoved change into the pocket.

I recognized her then, remembered having met her with Peter in the Lord Elgin or Finch's or Ward's; one of the Irish, English, Anglo-Irish, Irish-English who appeared to move between Dublin and London as freely as the gulls drifting with the mail boat. Peter had told me that she and Stephen had been lovers, that it had ended, but that they lived together still. 'For me'—sigh—'they will always be together.'

'We were just talking about Peter,' Stephen began.

'That shyster.' She turned to look around the bar, greeted a woman in white cord trousers standing, one boot on the rail, at the counter talking with a short cock-robin-chested man; turned back to us.

'So,' Stephen tried again, 'where have you been?'

'McDaid's.'

Stephen's studied cool faltered. 'Oh dear. Anyone there?'

'Just Jack,' Helen mimed with her cigarette, drawing it back and forth like a trombone slide, 'and Colin.' She drank off her unspilled wine, looked at me as I offered to buy another. 'What do you do?'

'I've left my job—'

'Again,' Stephen added.

Helen went to the counter again. This cult of generosity was new to me. 'What does she do?'

'Doctor.'

Different from the doctors I knew. I wondered if other journalists were like Stephen, then remembered that I had met another journalist—another piece of news. As Stephen turned to me again, looking as if he might say 'So …?' I remarked casually, 'Davis gave me a book to review the other day.'

'Did he now?'

Which led to another remark, conversation flowing now. 'I sent him a story. He wrote back offering me book reviews.'

'Oh dear. The consolation prize.'

'No, he accepted the story.'

'I see … So, what's the book?'

'It's about swans.'

Stephen laughed. I smiled with ruefulness as studied as his amusement.

'Swans!' He turned to Helen. 'Darling, he's reviewing a book about swans.'

Wonderful this glimpse between the great double doors. Wasn't it pleasant though to linger chatting on the threshold, from there steal further glimpses of that life beyond? Even more ruefully now, I was telling funny stories about the book I had to review: swans monogamous ... swans royal property ... status of swans in the Republic; slipping off to the Gents then, glancing at my watch—eleven already, the time going so easily; thinking up further harmless topics to take me to closing time. Returning to the bar, smiling at myself in the whiskey mirror ...

They were gone.

I stood stone cold, looking at the empty table. On the marble top—an empty pint glass, empty wine glass and my pint half-drunk.

Numb at the insult, but I savoured its justice as I sat sipping alone. My mind held only two ideas, joined yet distinct like a compass: Home, and Away from Home. Home was the hole made by the compass pin; Away was the circle the pencil described. Home was everything fixed, real, orderly, absolute, safe. Away was ... the image kept changing. Away was the ever-receding ripple from the pebble splash, Peter gasping on the circumference in London, the smoke from my old gate-lodge chimney floating into the blue. I had left that lodge but was still clinging to the compass pinhole. And so far as Stephen and Helen were concerned, I could stay there. Well I wouldn't. Never never never. I put down my empty glass and stepped out into the night. *Never.*

— 2 —

'Dear Kenny,
I shall be in town on business next Friday and wonder if
you would care to have luncheon with me? The Kildare
Street Club, 1.15 p.m.?
C.H.K. Daly.'

Good old Major Daly. A free lunch—and on Friday, lean end
of the week. I hurried down the quays to what I had left
behind.

Major Daly was a gentleman farmer who ran his estate
along the lines of the Victorian British army. 'Not there'—to
the labourer leaving a ladder back in the yard. 'There'—pointing to a spot six inches away. Eighty-six years old but still
about sixteen stone weight, he stood out even from the half-
dozen tall, slightly brutal-looking Anglo-Irish at the bar. He
called as he saw me 'Another Three Swallows', in a voice that
anywhere else would have brought the barman out over the
counter.

That was another reason for wanting to be with him. His
certainty was as reassuring to me as a gothic cathedral.

Eighty-six, but he still jumped into Lough Owel every day.
That was usually where our conversations had taken place, as I

wandered alone along the shore and met him coming out, water spilling from huge khaki shorts; and standing there knee-deep in the numbing cold he talked of a stoat he had seen or of his morning reading from the Bible.

'... Are you familiar with the Book of Daniel? You know—those beautiful lines where the King comes down to the lions' den and calls—*Daniel Daniel servant of the living God, is thy God whom thou servest continually able to save thee from the lions?*' Water-hens flapping away in fright as Major Daly called Daniel's reply across the lake—

'*OH KING! LIVE FOR EVER* ... What is there in modern literature to compare with that—Mmm?'

The business that had brought him to town today was a visit to the Museum. Putting down his whiskey, he took from each of his jacket pockets a bronze axe-head, placing one in my hand to be admired. A forebear had found them, they had been in the family ever since. But now he was getting on, he thought of presenting them to—that slightly brutal Anglo-Irish smile again—'The Nation.' Bronze Age by the look of them, pitted and dented, probably from smashing skulls, they lay on the tablecloth between us during lunch, as if illustrating Major Daly's argument, an old favourite: nothing important ever changes.

Shrewd enough in his own way, he had an arrangement with the Sligo line train drivers who, as they passed through his land every morning, threw out his copy of *The Times*—though he accepted that as a poor second to the days when they stopped the train for him. Today a story about Mick Jagger was on his mind.

First, there was the usual preliminary grind in new words—it reminded me of Peter's grinds in modern poetry.

'Look here, Kenny, what are *groupies*?'

'Girls who throw themselves at pop stars.'

'Ah.' He bent over his soup, showing the nut-brown wide

bald head. 'And'—looking up again, dabbing napkin on white moustache—'*roadies?*'

'They look after the pop group when it's on the road.'

'Of course. Of course.' He tore a bread crust gently apart.

'Some groupies throw themselves at roadies too,' I added.

'But only if they can't have the pop stars?'

'Probably.'

'Yes. I remember when I was on a column in Baluchistan …' He was off, face brightening, red plucks shining: nothing important ever changes. 'We'd arrive in some village for the evening, don't you know, and the head man would receive us for the night. Everything put at our disposal. The best food. The best places to sleep. The best girls offered—'

'Really? And would you—?'

Smile fading at my impertinence, Major Daly went on, 'But you never knew, you never quite knew. A wrong word or gesture and they'd as soon have taken your head off!' Smile returning. 'They looked so beautiful though, made one feel so plain, don't you know—those girls with their bright clothes rustling and their big eyes looking out over their veils. Of course if you'd seen their faces'—hearty laugh—'you'd probably have been sick!'

And now it was my smile's turn to fade. We looked awkwardly at each other, then down at the bronze axe-heads on the table. This was usually how our conversations ended: my strict verger ushering me out of that gothic cathedral back into the harsh everyday.

'I'm the most miserable creature on earth,' he had said the evening I left, when I called to return his gate-lodge key, said in the same curt way he ordered the labourer; stepping back then between the Ionic columns of his doorway and locking himself in for the night, as if for ever.

Turning this over in my head, and enjoying my lunch, I noticed a familiar face looking at me from the window table—Percy.

Percy was another ancient monument I hid behind, though to look at he was more like a water reed. Six foot tall, about eight stone weight, almost as old as Major Daly, he came swaying across the dining-room as if his knees might fold up in despair at any instant and drop him on the carpet. Major Daly glanced up at him, watery old eyes flickering like a fruit machine, registering the jackpot; Percy glancing down, registering maybe two lemons. Percy also came from the landed gentry, but had sold the land and given himself to writing. This had left him with strong feelings against people like Major Daly. 'The most ignowant bastards who ever lived,' he had lisped suddenly one day, two pinpricks of red coming up in his yellow face. That had been in the RDS. He must have belonged there—his bust was in the library—but that didn't stop him from stealing books, shoving them down into his raincoat pockets. In a similar way, he sauntered into places like this, the frail stare daring anyone to challenge him, but they never did—he so obviously belonged.

Introduced to Major Daly, he was the gentleman complete for a minute, at ease, chatting about nothing. Then he leaned over to me—'What are you doing after lunch, are you … fwee?'

I picked up one of the axe-heads, looked up at Major Daly. No help. I looked back to Percy. 'Major Daly is presenting these to the Museum. I—'

'Whatever you like,' Major Daly said huffily. 'I thought you might like to come along.'

'Where will you be, Percy?' To call Percy 'Mister', I realized, was as difficult as calling Major Daly 'Charlie'.

'I thought of going over to McDaid's.'

'It's two now …' I looked at my watch, feeling their eyes on my blushing face.

Youth: that was what they wanted, the youth that I was fleeing, wishing it and all its choices as deeply buried as the two bronze axe-heads had been.

'I may see you then—after the Holy Hour?' Percy stubbed

his menthol cigarette in our table's ashtray and wavered off towards the door.

'The *Holy Hour*,' Major Daly repeated, his fruit machine eyes flickering again, coming to rest in zero confusion.

Conversation dragged through the rest of lunch. Returning to the *Times* article on the Rolling Stones, Major Daly asked what marijuana was. I explained, and he recalled that when he had joined the Indian army opium was still part of a private soldier's ration. Nothing important ever changes. The idea was as reassuring as the Museum. Everyone, everything—art, manners, morals—had a place, as fixed as the torques, crosses, bronze swords in the glass cases.

The museum official led us past them, upstairs to his office, his face glazed with sycophancy, crooning gratitude to Major Daly for such a gift. I looked about the room as they talked: Bewley's cakebox hanging by red twine from hat-stand, Fox's briar pipe smouldering in Waterford crystal bowl, crisp folded *Irish Times*. I read its headline upside-down—the British embassy was moving to Merrion Road, their burnt-out house in Merrion Square was to be sold—while Dr Ó Fuaidh went on crooning about previous donations. The sun swung behind black and blue clouds and it was cold, swung out again and it was warm.

It had been a day like this, when my fairytale lodge felt more like a prison cell than usual, that I had run out the door and caught the crossroads bus to Dublin; got out when it was stopped at O'Connell Bridge by a crowd marching over; joined the march and saw it swell like an angry sprain until it was a mob when it reached Merrion Square; the railings swaying back, straightening again with the movement of the crowds; the blue block of Guards waiting for the order to baton-charge, relief showing on their white faces when no order came; the roar sinking as someone climbed to the embassy's first-floor window and smashed it with a hatchet; rising again, like the flames.

'... And I was out on Lambay Island, that's Lord Revelstoke's place, you know, Major, and we were strolling up and down when suddenly I noticed it—"Rupert," I said, "Rupert, do you realize that we're walking on *porphyry!*"'

The ribbon of some decoration in his buttonhole, ham-pink hands folded on his paunch, last waistcoat button left carefully undone—here was the fruit of Major Daly's never-changing world, I thought. Here was Major Daly himself, maybe, thirty or forty years ago, before old ivy blurred the hard edges. I thought of what he had said after Derry's Bloody Sunday—'If you annoy soldiers, you must expect trouble', words as hard smooth unanswerable as the old bronze axe-heads. Dr Ó Fuaidh was stroking them in gratitude as he stood up, shaking hands with Major Daly, giving me an old bishop's nod.

'Decent sort of ...' Major Daly's sunbrowned forehead wrinkled as he searched for a word, as we went down the museum steps '... beast.' He glanced up Kildare Street, waved down a taxi, thanked me for my company as it cruised to a stop alongside.

'Kingsbridge.' The chassis sank on its springs as he climbed inside.

'Do you mean Heuston?'

'Drive on!'

That was the last time he would invite me to lunch at his club. Battle done, axe-heads symbolically handed over, he was home to his house in the woods, while I was marching out.

A look at the companion Percy introduced as Colin, and I guessed it was the Colin Helen had mentioned. Then the figure drooped alongside would be Jack. The place was blue with smoke but it felt airy fresh after Dr Ó Fuaidh's office. The short cock-robin-chested man with a florid tie was standing at the counter, talking with the woman in boots and cord trousers—a bit dirtier now. And down in the back alcove—Stephen, his arm about Helen, her head sunk on her breast.

'Dearest divine ...' Jack murmured—gazing up at me, I thought; I sat down well away from him. He continued gazing upwards. '... Sarah'—he addressed the blue-veined air.

'Sawah who?' Percy enquired after a minute or two.

'Bernhardt,' Colin explained. An American accent.

More silence.

'Well, if she's there,' Colin paused for so long that I turned to look at him: butterfly bright bow tie, grey goatee waxed into two yellowish curls at the tips, 'I suppose he has to talk to her.'

'The face that launched a thousand quips.' Percy raised his little glass. 'Sláinte.'

Another silence. I looked about again and saw Pat, the old Donegal man from the Brazen Head, washing down a ham sandwich with red lemonade, ignoring a small dirty, dapper man standing beside him. Pat nodded as his eye met mine.

'Who *is* that,' Colin turned to me, 'with Laurence?'

'Who's Laurence?'

'There, seeking whom he may devour.' Percy gestured with his glass: the small man was turning away to buy an *Evening Press*, murmuring something, pressing a delicate dirty hand to the newsboy's cheek.

The noise blurred his words and a back-answer from the boy, who burrowed deeper into the crowd. Shoving the paper into his pocket, Laurence gazed up again at the slow-chewing mustard-smeared mouth.

'That's Pat,' I said. 'He lives in the Brazen Head.'

'The shilling kip.' Percy raised a hand as if to scratch his toupee, hiding his face as Laurence suddenly flapped past. The door swung shut. 'Yes, Laurence used to live down there.'

'What does he do?'

'He once wrote a ... Persian play.'

'He did too.' Jack was surprisingly awake. 'Two weeks in the Abbey.'

'What does he do now?'

'Why do you ask?' Jack turned a stare on me.

'I—' I side-stepped into the shelter of Colin's reply—

'Some shit-awful job. Kitchen porter, something like that.'

'He's not.' Pat took a single, long Guard's step to stand over our table. 'He's night porter below in the Talbot Hotel.'

'Weally?'

'Aye.'

'Hi!' Colin chimed in.

I did the introductions. Pat stood chewing, hands clasping his sandwich and lemonade, waiting till I had finished to say, 'And what's your name?'

I told him. I had told him before, and he would forget again.

(Back in the Brazen Head that night he would say to me, 'What're you doing drinking with that crowd for? They're only a pack o' queers.'

'Percy's not,' I would say hotly.

'Who?')

Now I said cockily, 'What're you doing here, Pat?'

'I meet a couple of the lads from home here sometimes. Aye, this was a great house for the Donegal men one time, back in old John McDaid's time. A Glenties man. Aye …'

That was how Pat seemed to spend his retirement, how he had spent his life in the city maybe: a desert nomad moving sure-footed from oasis to oasis—ten o'clock Mass in John's Lane, the Garda Club for dinner, tea in the Bórd na Móna canteen, then back to the Brazen Head; parleying with fellow nomads about the news from home, visiting alcoholic priests in St Pat's; as warily indifferent to Dublin as the nomad to the sands, eyes fixed on the next oasis.

'I'll go.' He buttoned up a heavy old gabardine the same colour as the mustard blob stuck to his lip. 'I have to go on down to Eason's for the *Democrat*.'

'Do that!' Colin's yawn was shrill.

'I will.' Pat spoke almost absently as he drew the belt tight into the buckle. 'I don't want any truck with you.'

'Oh … truck off!'

Percy practically laughed—as strange as if the foxy grin had appeared on that bronze bust of him in the RDS. The little row had lifted his spirits, now he wanted to prolong the mood.

Tamping down his nicotine-coloured toupee, picking a pound from his wallet, he went to the counter. Every week since he had sold the land he drew this allowance of mint green notes from the bank. As regularly for the past thirty years he typed up his journal. Showing me the bale of folders one day, he had raised his shoulders slowly into a shrug of total despair. There was only one way of—as he put it—*finishing* the journal: suicide. He rinsed the word about his mouth in the way Barrett said the word Home.

Returning with another dwy shewwy, he sat down slowly, section by section like trellis folding, lighting another Consulate, intoning:

'Twee things help me to bear the brunt—

Dwink and cigawettes and cunt.'

'Th th.' Jack frowned.

'You've got two ...' Colin glanced outside as July hailstones rattled on the window. 'Not bad.'

'Only one thing smells stronger than money,' Percy mused. 'Cunt.'

'I am ignorant of both.' Colin closed his eyes peacefully.

I was growing used to these pauses, sudden natural as the sky going from blue to black.

'*Soleil, je te viens voir pour la dernière fois* ...' Jack was addressing his cloud of cigarette smoke again, pale azure as the sun swung out.

'*Esther?*' Percy enquired.

'*Phèdre.*'

'Not again,' Colin's eyes stayed shut. 'How about a change of programme?'

'Racine—' Percy thought aloud. 'Did he write great literature? Or literature about great people?'

'Great literature about great people.'

'Can there be great literature about ordinary people?'

'Henry James said you can't write a good book about a poor rat.'

[37]

'He never read *Crime and Punishment*.'

'Nor *Wind in the Willows*,' Colin put in.

'I suppose it all depends on what you mean by *great*,' Percy went on. 'The King James Bible is *great* literature. I find the new versions just as good, better—but they aren't *great*.' Puff puff. 'But how could they be? Think of King James' time: nobles in furs, ladies with peacock feathers, peasants in moleskin—imitating the hierarchy of nature.'

'Moleskin! Mmm I can see myself in moleskin!' Colin pressed his skinny leg against mine. I moved away.

'In fact, is *great* literature good literature at all? Or just … *barbaric splendour*?' Percy turned to me. I edged further away. As if reminded of something, he looked at his watch and stood up. 'Can I hope to see any of you on Sunday evening at my—'

'At Home?' Colin yawned.

'Term of derision—yes.' Percy pushed out the door.

'Dwink and cigawettes,' Colin mimicked as the door swung shut, 'and now for cunt.'

'Th th.' Jack shut his eyes again. 'Th.'

At the end of the bench I sipped my pint alone. Again. I had gone to lunch with Major Daly—again gone back to that compass pin-hole. Been drawn from it by Percy, who had led me here, but again—

'Where have you been?' Stephen appeared, Helen leaning on his arm. 'We thought you'd gone back down the country.'

'Ha! Tell the truth.' Helen slipped from Stephen's arm, fell into mine, kissed my cheek. 'Come around for a drink some night. You know where we live.'

'Alright.'

She fell back into Stephen's arm and together they swung out the door.

— 3 —

The green baize card-table rickety under the typewriter's weight, the paper's white sheet, rain spilling down on Power's distillery, Maureen in the back yard sluicing out the toilets and warbling 'Delilah'. Morning peace.

First a quick piss. Then work. *Work.* Till evening. Till night. *Till dawn.*

Down the corridor I heard the bathroom geyser roar. I knocked. No reply.

'It's me.'

The door opened, Michael looked out with his humble grin. In a saucepan on the blazing geyser his weekly chicken boiled. The smell brought Maureen up at a run. Back in my room I waited for the row to end.

'Get that out of here before I throw it down the toilet!'

'Sure I never take a bath! Amn't I entitled to—'

Now—I dialogued calmly with myself—Where were we?

—Writing a novel.

—Fine. Now. Let's start at the beginning.

—I did.

—Fine, *fine*. So the young man has arrived in Dublin. Now, let's ask the simple question: What is he going to do?

—That's the question.

—Great. Now we're getting somewhere. Now we're at the station, so to speak. Now, and this is embarrassingly simple, Adrian: what are *you* going to do?

—I don't know.

—Jesus! Look—

—No, you look!

The dialogue in my head got louder, like the argument outside in the corridor.

'Do I have to go down for Mrs Cooney?'

'Sure it'll be done in a few minutes.'

'Mrs Cooney, would you ever come up here a minute!'

'Aw, you're mean as dirt.'

'At least I never cooked a chicken in a toilet.'

The telephone rang. Mrs Cooney called upstairs, 'Adrian!'

Percy again, asking me to support his At Home? Colin suggesting another meeting? I hoped not—last time he had suggested we 'go away together for the weekend'.

'Hello?'

'Where were you at all?' My mother.

My stomach knotted up. 'Upstairs.'

'Upstairs? What are you doing upstairs?'

'In my room. Writing.'

'Oh … of course I don't know what took you down there in the first place. That awful place. Who was that answered the phone?'

I took a slow breath, shot my never-fail Mama-stopper— 'How are you?'

Silence. 'Ah, alright, thank God.' Then: 'Will you come out to dinner this evening? We're having Kevin and Celia.'

'Alright.' Pause. 'I'd better let you get cooking!' Laugh. And I put down the receiver, fast.

★

Forty years since my father had come to Dublin—1932, the year his hero de Valera came to power—to a job in Frawley's of Thomas Street, to a room in the Brazen Head. Thirty years since he had opened his first shop—the small western farmer's son attacking a patch of city land watered by the money total war released. Opened a second, a third. Sat tight through the fifties, pushed out again in the sixties.

Now the small city farm was complete: half-a-dozen shops, each like a field with its own character, each known with the loving-hating intimacy hard labour brings. Capel Street was good for men's shoes, Grafton Street for women's, Stillorgan for children's; Camden Street, the rushy acre, was good for nothing; Northside needed more work.

There was an outlying acre too, a wholesale shoe business he had bought, keeping on the owner as manager. Old Mr Bennett was delighted with this. His own father had founded the firm, then laid it on his shoulders; now my father was taking the weight. When Noel, my older brother, was put in to learn the trade, Mr Bennett was even more delighted; fellow members of that great club, Reluctant Heirs, they sat at their desks chatting over the invoices about trout and salmon fishing.

There they all were—Noel, Kevin and his girlfriend Celia waiting in the sitting-room when I arrived, late—late, to assert independence, and because I feared these visits home. The warm austere house of childhood—lino in the study, tiles in the conservatory, a single fire fanned by draughts woo-wooing in under doors—had become a luxury hotel. Carpets everywhere, storage heaters throbbing out heat in the bedrooms, the beds made up ever-ready for our return; a book, left open on a bed-side locker months before, kept carefully open there. To me this was the cunning casual scatter of branches laid over a pitfall: one careless step and I'd find myself sprawling on my back down at the bottom of childhood.

'Well, Adrian.'

'Hello, father.'

I picked my way across the autumn-leaf carpet, sat into an armchair, turned with the others to watch TV golf, hiding with them in drives, chips and putts from the strain of Celia's presence. None of us had ever brought a girlfriend home to dinner before. The tension was exciting, but as exhausting as the heat coming out in waves from the big log-coal-briquette fire. Flamelight flashed from the family photographs along the mantelpiece.

From the corner of my eye I watched Celia scan these battlements. Thin, pale, pretty, she had the slightly hard, attractively quick expression of someone long used to looking after herself. She lived nearby in a bedsitter—my mother had stumbled at the word, hurried on to higher ground: 'She's a music teacher.'

She was from Scotland, Kevin had told me, introducing us a few months before. I had been in Major Daly's cottage when they arrived one Friday evening for the weekend. Together they had picked their way around cowpats as if they were landmines, held the candle as if it was a torch spilling wax everywhere, lain awake all night—she on the spare bed, he on the kitchen couch—calling to each other every time Major Daly's wheatfield crow-scarer exploded. It had rained all weekend. We had sat about the table, an old one from home, Kevin and I blowing on the fire of brotherhood, making small-talk. In the end I gave up, went up to Major Daly's house with some books he had lent me—already I was preparing to leave. But he had been out and I returned to find my cottage door locked. I knocked. No reply. More knocking. I stood in the downpour of rain until Kevin appeared in my dressing-gown, his face shining with embarrassment and delight. No sign of Celia. My bedroom door shut.

So he had succeeded, on the very bed where I had failed; where Vivienne had lain, country pink face smiling as she mopped from between her thighs my spunk shot off before I had even entered her. But how could anyone, unless he was cold as ice, contain himself long enough to—

[42]

'It's because you just want to get it over with, say it's nothing'—her sharp answer the thorn that had finally driven me out of the fairy-tale cottage. I had left the old table behind.

The new table was antique, a rosewood oval, hidden this evening by dishes. My mother was hiding in kitchen-work from the strain, no maid now forcing freedom on her; my father was busying himself opening a bottle of wine, filling our glasses with the relish of the ex-drinker. His own bottle of Jung's alcohol-free wine was still on the sideboard, three-quarters full, and the box of cigars still brim-full. His role as Successful Businessman had been a flop, folded after a disastrous first night of self-conscious sipping and puffing. He poured himself a glass of Seven-Up, heard the doorbell ring and with obvious relief hurried out of the room.

'I'll just shut this door to keep the steam in ...' My mother locked herself in the kitchen.

Noel, Kevin and I made you-know-how-it-is smiles to Celia, who smiled, said, 'I know how it is.'

The direct translation brought silence. It was alright for us to smile at our parents, but a smile from an outsider made us withdraw, head, feelers and all, into the family shell. A strange shell: without the carapace of the established middle class we had moved into, without the toughness of the peasant class we had left behind. The room reflected our class: a girl in a bikini pouting from a postcard behind the Sacred Heart lamp; a Wedgwood bowl; a candle burning before a bust of the Virgin Mary, the blue box of Antacid tablets alongside.

The door opened again, my youngest brother, Brian, came in, breaking the silence with—dismal attempt at a Dublin accent—'So when's the wedding?'

On the run from family prosperity, he was living with the Simon Community on Ellis Quay; pasty-faced-pimpled from poor food, dressed in jersey and jeans, with aggressively poor shoes, he took his place.

'Why spoil a beautiful relationship?' Celia smiled.

Encouraged by the sound of conversation, my father return-ed, dishcloth on wrist, and served an egg mayonnaise.

Behind the calm waiter's face—the anxious father's face. Behind that—power. Father power, energy power, money power, good-looks power; as impossible to hide or disown as love, twisting to the surface sometimes in a glance or gesture, suggested in other smothered ways—his padding down to the kitchen at night, say, like a lion to the water hole, lowering a pint of raw orange juice in one hoarse unbroken swallow.

Tailored grey chalkstripe suit, red socks—in case any old Anglo types think he was imitating them—blowing a raspberry at it all, some silvered hair sleeked back either side of a high bald forehead darkened by golf-course sun, burnished black brogues creaking gently, he moved about the table to Celia.

'No, thanks.' Her voice not aggressive, not defensive. Cool. It made a shocking wavelet of silence, rippling outwards, push-ing open the kitchen door—and behind my father appeared my mother, the rock on which he had pitched his pavilion.

'I forgot the lemon.' She set it on the table, eyed Celia's plate, as clean as Kevin's.

Kevin: hater of the egg since infancy. 'Look at the little man on the ceiling,' my mother would say, and as he looked up she would shove a spoonful of egg into his mouth; but Kevin would spit it out. Kevin: tearer-off of strips of wallpaper. Kevin: mitcher. Kevin: 'not academic'. Kevin: flogged for stealing two shillings from the maid … Kevin now his father's dearest disci-ple, following him devoted into the family business, imitating his turns of speech. But not this evening. He turned to Celia and, as if catching a tonic note, said in a light firm voice, 'Celia doesn't like egg mayonnaise either.'

'Oh,' my mother said. Then: 'You could share Kevin's smoked salmon. Would you like that, Celia?'

'Yes, please.' Not aggressive, not defensive. Cool.

The house rules for dealing with strangers hadn't changed.

With relations we were relaxed and bored, with strangers we enjoyed ourselves and were on guard. With Celia we were both. One minute we were talking with her about Jamaica, the next about Kevin's asthma. It was like mixing drinks—elating but confusing. She explained that she had been an air hostess once—

'With what airline …?' My father, as if trying but failing to utter her Christian name, left the sentence in mid-air.

Celia said she had been with Aer Lingus, even though she was from the UK. She pronounced it Yew Kye. Kevin said that was the way things should be. Brian asked if there were many Irish hostesses with British Airways, my mother interrupted to say that last spring she had flown with Dada to London for the Shoe Fair.

Celia nodded, 'Kevin was telling me.' And we talked about shoes, treading warily now, as if some other deep pitfall lay beneath these familiarities with strangers.

Given the precise time of birth, an astrologer will cast a horoscope. Given the right information, we might predict the spouse another will take. But what is the right information?

Nothing so superficial as hobbies, interests. In Kevin's case, symbolic hatred of the egg; his smothered rebellion put down, his adult manner a stencil copy of his father's—the identical dismissive shake of the head, the same calm phrases—convincing until you saw the emptiness underneath; his new flat in Waterloo Road, for instance—anonymous and bare as a hospital room except for a cartwheel-sized straw sombrero on the wall, only souvenir of his only holiday abroad, proclaiming in a yellow cry—'Doesn't fit! Too big for me!'

What more natural match for him than Celia? Celia from the Yew Kye but living in Rathmines, an outsider at home; as tough beneath her waif's face as Kevin was a waif beneath his tough face; the specially respectable clothes she wore this evening disguising, at the same time somehow proclaiming, something very different underneath.

[45]

What did my father make of us? Of me as I addressed him 'Father'—part of my plan to establish formal, adult distance—and talked with him as if conducting a TV interview? Of Noel, eldest son, evading a business question, smiling as Kevin answered the question and then turned to explain it to Celia, who nodded and dabbed genteelly a crumb from brown sheer-stockinged thigh? Of Brian standing up as coffee appeared, excusing himself with a brusque 'I'm on the soup run tonight'?

Celia observed that he was doing wonderful work. My father nodded and frowned; hooded, pouched eyes narrowing in concentration as he trickled cream over the back of a spoon onto each cup of coffee and passed it down the table. He hadn't grown rich for nothing. Whatever about his family, he was going to enjoy some of his labour's fruits, the rituals of the senses: gargling Floris mouthwash, rubbing Bay Rum in his hair, alcohol spirit into the palms of his hands—supposedly toughening them for golf; inhaling Friars Balsam; slipping into the Seventh Day Adventist Church in Ranelagh where he had discovered a Turkish Bath and a masseur; into the Green Dolphin too, where the barber laid a hot-steamed towel over your face; buying pungent cheese and coffee; flirting with hand-made shirts. All this and more—a taste for Meissen, Venetian glass—simmering under that austere-angled jaw.

'What do you think of that? That's Mount Kenya with—I asked him to mix in a little Java.' His face looked up, for a moment off-guard, and I caught in the slightly red-rimmed clouded blue eyes a hungry far-away pleading poor boy's look.

'It's lovely, Dada!' I said. Under the table I drove fingernails into my palms. Dada!

Afterwards Celia was persuaded to play the piano, singing 'Loch Lomond', then a wee aria from *West Side Story*.

'I feel pretty, oh so pretty—' My mother joined in as she gathered up the coffee cups and then moved with speed back to the kitchen. To the muffled beat of the dishwasher, Celia played the Humming Chorus from *Madame Butterfly*.

'Well, I could listen to that forever.' My mother's head appeared at the service-hatch, drew back out of sight.

Always during these visits home my stomach remained knotted, yet in the end—in the way insomniacs fall suddenly asleep—I relaxed, found myself ... at home. And then—as insomniacs snap awake—I was alert again, waiting for the right, casual cue to take my leave. The broken ormolu clock chimed ten. I glanced at my watch and rose as if reluctantly slowly. My father went with me to the hall.

'Have you a moment?' He led the way into the study.

Now there was no one to use it, he had taken over this room for himself. Golf trousers hanging from bookshelves above the storage heater. Spikes of dockets on the desk. He sat down, turned the chair to face me, as awkwardly as he had puffed the cigar and sipped the Jung wine. 'About your new job in the telephone exchange—'

'It's well-paid.' I had been expecting that.

'What are the hours like?'

'Five in the evening till one in the morning.'

'Well, that's an honest day's work.'

'I write in the day.'

'How's that going?'

Dire. 'Fine, father.'

'Now, I'm not an old man, but I'm not young either. So I'm beginning to—kkm!—set my affairs in order.' He coughed on the phrase, as he had coughed when the cigar smoke had gone down the wrong way.

'*I belong to Glasgi, dear oold Glasgi toon. There's someing the maher wi Glasgi, for it's going roond an roond ...*' Celia's music-teacher voice carried across the hall. My father shut the door.

'Now, Noel and Kevin have the business—they're alright. Brian won't take anything, as you know, and if he did he'd give it away, so maybe that's just as well. I'll talk to Phil when she comes back from London. Now, what I've drawn up for you ...' He turned back to the desk.

[47]

The small city farm was flourishing now, all the digging, manuring and fencing done; like trim ricks, sleek livestock, the chequebooks and passbooks—Bank of Ireland, Lombard and Ulster, Guinness Mahon—lay on the maroon desktop. I had glanced at them sometimes, seen frightening four- or five-figure sums, and looked away. Now I had to look straight at them. I stood leaning over my father's shoulder in his aroma of Bay Rum, nodding as the long heavy finger moved down the accountant's typed figures.

'But I don't need that sort of money, father.'

'That's alright. Don't touch it. Leave it. It'll be accumulating. Take the interest if you need it. You look at fellows like old Bennett, those old Protestant businessmen—they're very very reluctant to touch their capital. You see,' his fingertips tap-tapped on the white paper, as if to the time of Celia's singing, 'I don't want you to be repeating this, but I've signed the business over to Noel and Kevin. I'm out of it now. And you notice it straightaway—the travellers pass me by now, the reps—they walk past me, they make for Noel or Kevin. They sense it. *They sense it* ... Money—money is something that has to be handled very very carefully. It's not everything, it's not everything. But it helps. As my mother used to say—If you've a shilling you'll always get something. Now'—he got up, put down the sheet of paper—'that'll be in your account on Monday morning.' He opened the door and across the hall again came the singing—

'But when Ah geh a coople o drinks on a Saherday, Glasgi belongs ta me!'

− 4 −

'To argue with his father was unimaginable. He was like a feudal baron dutifully collecting from his vassals huge tithes and taxes (in this case of will and consciousness) for some far-off ruler who never himself appeared …'

What a monster this father was! On a stiff white card—which just fitted between the side of the typewriter and the edge of the table—I wrote 'Father: ruthlessly weak.'

The card was full of these good lines, cut stones to be fitted into the great structure—

'His father—a sunken ship through whose wreckage the sons swim like fishes.'

And warnings—

'No arty stuff. This is real.'

'Nothing must happen. No characters. No plot.'

But why must nothing happen? Why no characters, no plot? How could you finish a novel without them? Because—I walked up the sloping floor to the window, looked out. I couldn't answer. But it would be like that evening at home in the study when, standing beside my father in his scent of Bay Rum, looking at the accountant's sheet of paper, I had gone rigid for an instant, stared, as it seemed for a moment that the figure his finger touched was rising off the page into … the *actual* sum—

Easy, take it easy.

—which was now deposited in my bank account. I sat down again, checked my watch, which just fitted between left side of typewriter and edge of card table. Eleven o'clock already.

Work.

Work. Across the Liffey my brother Brian was already making up old men's beds. Kevin was shooting about town from shop to shop. Noel was sitting in South William Street checking invoices and chatting with old Mr Bennett. All busy about our father's business ... Yes, even Brian—because wasn't that what his work with old men was really about? He had even adopted one of the down-and-outs, an old whiskey jockey; took him out, sat with him all night in terrible pubs. But wasn't it really the other way round—that Brian needed the old man? In fact—I got up again, walked uphill to the window—what was my novel about except the old man? Oh my God! What else was my life except the old man's?

—How do you mean?

—Where have you just come from?

—A cottage in Westmeath.

—And who else came from a cottage in the West? And moved into the Brazen Head? And worked worked worked?

—The old man! I'm just re-enacting my father's life. Prolonging my life as my father's son.

That was it. We were all at it, like water caught in the channel our father had made, lapping against his dam, falling back and eddying in circles. Well, I wouldn't. *I wouldn't.*

—Go on then. Who's stopping you?

—Go on where?

—Wherever you want. What do you want to do?

—I just want to finish this book and then—

—Fuck the book! Go on, get out of here. *Live.*

—I can't. Not until I finish this.

—Why? *Why?*

★

I rang the bell, looked up as a top-floor window-sash screeched open. Stephen's head appeared. Down dropped a sock, a key in the toe. I let myself into a hall empty as a shell. Bare walls except for numbers scribbled about a pay-phone on the landing. Bare stairs narrowing flight by flight to step-ladder size at the top.

Stephen and Helen were in opposite armchairs, drinking wine, smoking dope and listening to a Van Morrison record—

The love that loves to love to
Say goodbye to Madame George ...

—half-closed eyes gazing at a ceiling splashed orange by the street light.

'Well, young Kenny.' Stephen drew deep on the joint, held it out to me. Helen swayed her way to the kitchen, came back with a beer glass of red wine. As hospitable as home, the opposite of home. Cold ashes flowing from the grate across the hearth, old plates unwashed on the floor, glass-rings like doilies everywhere, the table's heap of books and bottles like a stage-set denoting chaos.

From this assertive Bohemia Stephen set out each morning to his newspaper office, Helen to her hospital, returning each evening to ritualized disorder: dinners of Carlsberg Special and spaghetti, strolls down to Grafton Street bars, returning late with a bottle of wine—the stage they had now reached.

A small exception to all this was a memoriam card on the mantelpiece with a stamp-sized photo of Stephen's father who, I would later learn, had died when Stephen was a boy. Blown off by draughts when the window was opened to throw down the key, or brushed off by elbows leaning on the mantel, it was always found somehow and propped once more against the chimney-breast, yet never referred to.

Helen on the other hand spoke freely of her father—'the old ballocks'—still alive and drinking, another of that strange tribe,

[51]

Irish doctors practising in England. So peasant-mean, she said, that he had rationed the radio when they were children, so peasant-proud that he had sent her to the best schools. Helen had put the Irish Sea between her and him but had held on to her public-school vowels. Yet quoting some remark of her mother's, her voice ran into a Cavan accent as strong as Michael's in the Brazen Head. Her face had the slightly severe look you see in people strictly loyal to origins they have left behind. I felt at ease, at home amongst my own—the nouveau riche. Well, almost.

After a few brimming glasses I spilled the news about my father's allowance.

'Squander it,' Stephen said.

'How?'

'Put it on a horse.'

'It might win,' Helen put in.

'Live off it, give up your job. God knows why, but you want to write, don't you.'

'I want to earn my living. I've enough time to write as it is.'

'I have to earn my living.' Stephen went to look at the alarm clock in the kitchen.

'I want to earn my living,' Helen mimicked. 'Why are you so middle-class?'

'I just want to be independent.'

'So if I gave you money you wouldn't mind?'

'No.'

'Give me a kiss.' She traced a target X on her cheek, then turned so her lips met mine.

'You just want to be able to get it out of the way, say it's nothing,' Vivienne had said. So far it had been nothing. This was something: Helen lying back, wine-black mouth drawing my tongue in to hers. A cough from the door. Helen didn't look up, nor I. Here was Bohemia: Stephen drying his face with a dish-cloth as he stood watching us; going back to the kitchen, busying himself with the drinker's night rites—setting a pub pint glass of water by Helen's bed, another for himself, a third brought in for me. He set it on the floor by the couch, stood watching again as Helen's hands went under my shirt, as mine went under her blue silk dress. Here was beauty too. No bra. Breasts surprisingly big and warm. No sound except the sound of our breath, the slap of her breasts meeting as she turned from side to side, the sound of the traffic down Leeson Street as the clubs emptied. Then Stephen said in a casual voice, 'Well, I'm off to bed, darlings.' No reply, and he added, 'Sleep here, if you want.' That was for me? For us? His bedroom door closed. There was a see-saw pause—dither-dither—my hands breaking no new ground, Helen's body falling still. She sat up slowly, drawing a brown veil of hair from her face, smiled and swayed through the door to her own bed. I slept on the couch, relieved it had gone no further, delighted it had gone so far, angry when I woke in the morning that it had gone no further.

I woke at the sound of Stephen moving about and went to the kitchen for more water, made some morning greeting sound.

'You're a funny little cunt, aren't you.' He put his teacup in the sink, put on Helen's gabardine and went down the stairs. The halldoor slam shook through the house.

So he wanted her still. And she didn't want him? I wandered about the flat, glanced now and then through the doorway at Helen's sleeping child's face—at odds with one bare breast showing above the tumbled bedclothes. Did I want her? Did she want me? I washed, dressed, read a poem half finished in Stephen's typewriter. I liked it. I read it again. I didn't like it. I ran tiptoe downstairs, out into clear morning air. *Live* ...

Mrs Cooney allowed some lodgers the use of her kitchen, or at least didn't forbid them.

'What are you going making?'

'An omelette.' I moved about on tiptoe to show I wasn't taking anything for granted.

'Lord save us.'

'Do you know the best meal of all?' Pat standing as usual under the light bulb.

Mrs Cooney ignored him, leaned through her cigarette smoke, watching as I greased the black iron pan. 'Is that butter?'

'Badger,' Pat said. 'Pig badger.'

'Hare-soup.' Michael spoke up from the end of the table. 'That's the best feed of all. Jugged hare, they do call it in England.'

'And you just pour it into the pan?' Mrs Cooney got up to look.

'That's all.' I turned it over, turned it out onto my plate.

'Oh the Englishman knows how to eat, I can tell you. A jug of mugged hare.' Michael shook his head clear. 'A mug of jugged hare. A lot better than this tack.' Washing down fish and chips with stout, putting hand in pocket again. 'Could I have another bottle, ma'am?'

'Oh the Englishman's grand,' Pat waited for Mrs Cooney to go into the bar, 'until it comes to mickeying. They go daft then.'

'They got a right doing there in Armagh last night—hah?' Michael counted change onto the table.

'They did, and I hope they get more. Blow the fuckers to kingdom come.'

I ate my omelette and hurried out, delayed outside the door as usual to hear what they said.

'What's that fella doing here at all?'

'Arra, he's harmless.'

What was I doing there? I stepped into the street. Already in six months a new generation of down-and-outs had sprung up. I was still there, hiding in that hole in the wall. The red-faced man who lay on his back drinking Marie Celeste and roaring had vanished. In his place now, a man with a fresh flower in his buttonhole every day, standing this evening on the parapet of Winetavern Bridge. A passer-by stopped, called up to him, 'Go on, do it. Jump, you fucker!' Turned to me then, 'Half mad, my eye. Half sane more like it. He won't take too many bites out of the wall, I can tell you. Come here till I tell you … COME HERE!'

I cut across Wood Quay. But wasn't that me—that dandy tramp on the parapet? Afraid to jump. But jump where? Into Parliament Street. Anywhere. Down Dame Street. Why? Up George's Street to Exchequer Street. Just jump.

Just in time, I signed my name in the book: half past five to midnight in the telephone exchange.

Returned to live in Dublin—but in the Brazen Head, a country kitchen. Writing a novel—but insisting it be fact. Clocking in to work—that my father's allowance had turned into play. But wasn't all that inevitable? Without a clear purpose, everything must be confusion. I put on my headset, plugged into a thousand voices.

'Yes, please?'

'Hello, Dublin. Derry 54042 please.'

'Hold the line, Shillelagh.'

An operator further down the board laughed aloud at some call he was listening to.

'Connecting you now, Shillelagh … Hello, Derry?'

'No.' Click.

I dialled again. 'Hello, Derry?'

The same sharp Northern 'No.'

'Sorry, I'm dialling the Derry code. What are you?'

'Londonderry.'

'Well, could I have 54042, please?'

'Where's that?'

'Derry 54042 is what I was asked for?'

'We've no such place here.' Click.

I switched back to the caller, got back abuse so loud it brought the supervisor to my side—Matt who had manned the door the night a caller drove in from Foxrock with a big stick. He glided my headset onto his head and murmured, 'Hello, caller?'

'What's your name? I want to make a complaint!'

'The name's Brown ...'

'Don't say Brown—' the chorus rose along the switchboard '—say Hovis!'

'Ah, lads,' Matt pressed a hand over the mouthpiece. 'Lads, will ye take a few calls.'

I plugged in again. 'Yes?'

'Hello, I'd like to make a personal call.'

'To whom, please?'

'Cardinal Conway.'

'*Cardinal Conway?*'

'Cardinal Conway ...' Along the board others plugged in to my call.

'Connecting you now ...'

'Hello. Cardinal Conway?'

'Yeiss?'

'You don't know me, but my name's Conway too ...'

'I've a better one.' Bill sitting alongside nudged me, whispered, 'Plug into thirty-seven.' He shut his eyes again, rapt.

'Thirty-seven ... thirty-seven ...' The word went down the board.

'I wish you were here now.'

'Mm. Me too. I wish you were here sucking my cock.'

'Mmm.'

'What're you wearing?'

'That greeny dress you bought me. Why?'

'Pull it up ...'

'Ah, lads, lads. Take a few calls for God's sake, the board's lighting up like Christmas.' Matt picked his teeth uneasily with his Pioneer pin.

'Hello, Derry? I want Londonderry 54042.'

'My grandmother was Katie Conway from ...'

[56]

'Are your knickers down?'

'Connecting you now, Shillelagh.'

A break at nine o'clock.

'Do ye want your Casual?'

'Thanks, Matt.' At least I was clear about that. I wanted to be across the street and into The Castle, where Stephen and Helen and the rest were drinking now. No longer 'the rest'— the faces had names now. The short cock-robin-chested man was Jamie. The woman in white cords and boots was Kate. Colin and Jack were there getting drunk, Bibby with a new boy, and Percy with another book in his raincoat pocket. Twenty-, forty-, fifty- and seventy-year-olds sitting at the same table: that was what I liked about this bar with its Expelair fan coated in brown greasy fluff.

'Well, Percy.' I leaned across the table: it was like another telephone exchange here, different conversations crossing. Helen talking with a handsome tall young man, Jonathan—she had noticed him one night in Neary's, now he was drinking here; Stephen leaning across to hear what they were saying. I raised my voice, 'Percy, what're you reading?'

Puff. 'Tonight—Newman.'

'Cardinal Newman? Why?'

Pause as he dipped his huge-pored nicotine-coloured nose into the sherry glass. I looked around, saw down in the lounge my brother Noel and old Mr Bennett. In the evening after work they strolled across South William Street to sit here chatting like happy father and son. Percy raised his glistening nose. 'He wanted to dream the true dream.'

Yesyesyes. 'How do you mean?'

'The fairytale'—puff—'which philosophy could not philosophize'—pause—'nor poetry poeticize away ...'

'Speaking of true dreams,' Stephen had given up, tuned into our conversation, 'is that Barrett I see?' He nodded across the bar.

[57]

Who else could it be? Standing like a heron, mournful sharp eyes transfixing some friend, looking at any moment likely to flap his long grey coat sleeves and glide out the door.

'Still in London, is he?'

'No, he's back. Down in Cork.'

'Still dodging Daddy,' Jamie smiled.

'I hear of him,' Percy caught the interest as others plugged in. 'Who is he?'

'A poet,' Jack said. 'And I mean a real poet.'

Percy gazed at Barrett with an old man's open childish stare, and sighed. 'All I could have learned if I'd talked to my father …'

'Did you not?'

'He would come into the room. And I would run out.'

'Why?'

Puff, pause.

'*Suidhe an athar i dthig a mhic*
A dhá glúin fá n-a smig;
Suidhe an mhic i dthigh an athar
A chosa sgartha trasna an teallaigh.'

'Nice to hear Irish with an Oxford accent.'

'Cambridge, actually.' Percy worked his lips up into a smile.

Grating of chairs and gulping of pints as other operators saw the time. The Casual was over. I stood up, stopping before Barrett. 'Peter—'

'Adrian …' Words-cannot-express sigh, eve-of-Waterloo handshake. And behind that? I scanned the hawk face, the pale scar like a blaze on one high cheekbone. Was it possible that he too was dodging Daddy?

'You're back?'

'Yes.'

'Why?

'Why should I hide like a rat in a hole in London?' His voice was angry. He pushed his way to the counter, indifferent to all about him: my brother still talking about angling with old Mr Bennett; Stephen leaning across the table to Helen and

Jonathan; Percy translating his Irish proverb for Colin—
  ' "The father sits in his son's house
With his knees up under his chin;
The son sits in his father's house
With his feet stretched across the hearth."
It's about *power*.'

A glimpse of the stars—Castor and Pollux way above Wicklow Street, Mars a gold spark just below—then into the exchange again. Another few hours at the switchboard lights, connecting and disconnecting voices that came out of the dark, thinking about my novel—until:

'Alright, lads, that'll do.' Matt stuck his Pioneer pin back in his lapel.

Dark night outside, shot through with star stabs of hysteria. Some Special Branch young men in bulging sportscoats, as if training for an important football match, kicked-fisted, ranroared someone into the back of a unmarked car. A tall, grey-haired-distinguished man walked along the path driving his fist into each parked car's headlamp, gazing at his bleeding fist in wonder. A woman, black-haired, white-faced, red-lipped, swayed to no-music in Nicholl's doorway, chanting 'Say a prayer for Bey.'

'Who's Bey.' I stopped. Again.

'Me.' She opened her arms, bag in one hand, Baby Power in the other, closing them about me in embrace. 'Say a prayer for Bey.'

Giving lips opening to mine, tobacco and whiskey sweet tongue sliding in, sliding out, handbag strap sliding up her arm as she sank down into my arms; cold cold hands underneath my clothes pressing my skin; cold cold breasts warming under my hands. She pressed her belly to mine, leaned back against the plate-glass.

'Hi, Murt!' A Special Branch roar carried through the frosty air. 'Here's another of the cunts!'

Mush! of something soft against steel shutters down the

street, a pain-scream, the slam of car-doors and screech-away of tyres.

'Say a prayer for Bey …' She vanished, a spark into the dark.

Who? I walked up Exchequer Street, into Dame Street. Where? And up Lord Edward Street … a waterworks man listening to his rod, to underground whisperings. How? Across Christchurch Place and down St Audeon's Steps … a man without his trousers, his nose running blood, standing at the postern gate sobbing, 'The fucker … the fucker …'

'What—?'

'Fuck off, you!'

And up Cook Street. A car cruised by, a new toilet bowl gleaming white in the back seat, and a hair-oiled head leaned out the window. A Cavan–Monaghan voice quietly called, 'Are you rambling?'

'Why?' I recoiled from the inviting smile, averted eyes.

'You're alright, you're alright.' The red tail-lights crawled away, leaving me to cross Bridge Street into the Brazen Head.

The sign's anonymous face—who where how what why?—gazed down as I slipped inside.

No need for a key tonight. A busy night tonight. Special Branch men soaking up the whiskey, old regulars discoursing on the cut-stone-work of Christchurch arch, the rules of Nap, the ingredients of coddle. Mrs Cooney leaned through the smoke, handed me a stiff white envelope. 'A young chap left this in for you.'

Knees still trembling after my nightly linger on the threshold of Life, I opened it: an invitation to my brother Kevin's wedding. I ran a finger over the raised black print. Things were starting to feel real.

− 5 −

Lying in the couch wet with sweat from my latest psychosomatic flu, listening to Helen and Jonathan make love again behind the varnished plank wall, to Stephen and his latest girl make the mattress twang—I heard the phone ring. Dripping with self-pity too, I went down the stairs.

'Adrian?'

'*Dada?*'

'Yes, I rang the Brazen Head and they told me—'

I looked out the dirty landing window at snow fall on a hundred chimneypots.

'… So I'll be starting off about one,' my father said.

'Where to?'

'It's a bad line. To Donegal. Can you hear me?'

'Yes.'

'Where are you?'

'Leeson Street.'

'Will I meet you on the bridge?'

Upstairs in Stephen's kitchen, I whistled with the kettle, raised five cups from the grey brimming sink. I was on the run again, but since it was my father's doing I needn't take the blame.

The sight of Stephen's girl, of Stephen's stubbled jaw set in discontent, cheered me even more.

'This is Pearl.' Stephen took his tea.

'Morning, Pearl!'

Pearl sat up, one hand drawing up the sheet, the other moving as quickly to touch her hair, silvered reddish, the sort—my weasel eye noted—that spoke of unhappy hours before the mirror.

'How are the other pair?' Stephen looked indifferent.

'Sitting up now, doing yesterday's crossword.'

'Tell them I'll be up in a minute.'

'I'll be gone.'

'Oh?' Stephen sank lower as Pearl chirped, 'Sure we'll see you again!'

Leaving his door wide open, to let in Helen's bubbly laughter, I let myself out and skipped downstairs.

From the front steps I could see my father's car gleaming on the hump of the bridge. I walked slowly to arrive, as I had said, at one. He looked at his watch. Aged about sixty, looking about fifty, acting about seventy. Where was the hysterically calm tyrant of my childhood? The father whistling in the riggings as the storm blew about his little business? Where was the deep peace after a good Saturday's trade, when the whole family exhaled? Who was this millionaire fusspot tuning in every hour to radio news he didn't listen to? Filling each spot of silence with small-talk, he steered along the South Circular Road, drawing in breath at each flurry of snow by way of further small-talk.

'It'll be bad in Donegal.' I made my contribution.

'If it gets worse, we can stop the night with Margaret. We'll see what it's like in Mullingar.'

Over twenty years, driving west with my father had become a ritual with its own lines. 'We'll have lunch in the Greville'; 'The old Shannon' as we rattled over Tarmonbarry bridge; 'Dear Jesus' to the rushes and furze of Mayo. But now his old home was no longer the destination. Having signed his business over to my brothers and found himself out of the game, he had bought an old schoolhouse in Donegal, high above Mulroy Bay,

to convert into a holiday home. 'It'll be an interest for me …'—
trying to stress the 'me', going on to describe the far-off eyrie
he was making for himself, where he could not bear to be
alone, where he was bringing me.

'You've had enough of the Brazen Head?' Pause, glancing
nod to great gates as we climbed Lucan Hill, 'That was Fr
O'Conor's home.'

'Really? Yes, more or less.'

'It was never much of a place.'

'The Brazen? You stayed there, didn't you?' I pointed casually as we passed Crowe's timber yard. 'He bought the trees
around my old gate-lodge.'

'Is that so? Yes, when I came to town first. Myself and Boysy
Delaney.'

'Did Boysy die?'

'He did, he did.'

'He drank—' I fiddled with the heater.

'He drank. Just slide the knob across. Too much, no more
than myself.'

'Why did you?'

'Oh, once I started, I had to have the whole bottle. That's
it—just slide it across.'

Lovely warmth. A small expensive car, the engine ticking
like a small clock, a dashboard of greenlit dials, wipers murmuring back, forth as the snow fell more heavily.

'Who were you staying with in Leeson Street?' He wiped
the windscreen with a shammy rag.

'Stephen.' By now he would be down in Neary's drinking
with Helen and Jonathan. 'Stephen Staunton.'

'I haven't heard you mention him? Married—' checking
that the choke was in '—is he?'

'No. Do you know his mother? She's a TD.'

'I do.' His face cleared. Fianna Fáil could do no wrong.
'And I knew her husband—a nice little man he was too. I can-
vassed for him.'

Lovely warmth spreading, the warmth of confidences ex-changed; the side windows white-papered with snow, making the car within like a cocoon.

'He doesn't mind you staying with him?'

'No, he has a spare bed.'

'Because you can always stay in Donegal, you know.' Putting his foot down a little, the engine's clock-tick no louder. 'Or with Margaret ...' Glancing at the sky. 'What do you think—will we stop the night in Knockshinny?' Laugh. 'Or you can stay with Petie for a few months. Oh, and I meant to tell you, we've an empty flat over the shop in Capel Street now, if you're interested ...'

That smothering family 'we' again. I changed the subject coldly. 'Why are you going to Donegal this time of year?'

'I'd like to have a look at the fireplace. They want to build it with granite, but I don't know if that's a good idea. You can tell me what you think of it.'

'OK.' I imposed a nominal punishment of ten minutes silence. Looking out at the trees, chalk-white against a slate sky, I thought of Stephen again. How could he pick up girls so easily? Philippa ... Heather ... Pearl. Handsome too. Usually. Why drop them then? Because he wanted Helen. Although he had seemed to like Heather until—there were post-mortems in the pub next morning when the girl had gone—Helen had called her an amiable cow. But then compared with Helen—primed by a Carlsberg Special, at the centre of attention—everyone was dull. And yet, without attention Helen could be dull, sulky, a coal going grey on the hearth. Now it was Jonathan's turn to blow on it till it glowed. Was that why she liked him—because he was on his knees before her? Or because of his—glimpsed as he sauntered naked back from the bath-room—huge cock? Hardly that, for Helen mocked sex. She would be mocking Stephen's latest last-night antics now, and he would be laughing, embarrassed, looking at her lying against Jonathan's heavy shoulder.

But all the time I was aware of the silence at my own shoulder, waiting for me to speak. 'I gave up my job,' I said. 'In the telephone exhange.' Calm.

'You didn't like it?' Calmer.

'It was alright.'

'And what will you do now? ... Look, look at him.' Casual nod at a fox, a rust streak across a field of snow.

'I used to hear them when I was in Major Daly's lodge.' Innocent? Perverse? I barked breath backwards down my throat—'I did that one night and four of them came running around the garden.'

Patiently: 'By the same token, I saw a house you might like. I was walking down Stephen Street the other day—'

'Where's this that is?'

'There off South William Street. Phil Fitzsimons is selling it—that's what caught my eye. So I gave him a ring—'

'Oh I don't think so, Dada.'

'It's up to you now. Have a look at it anyhow, next time you're passing. There beside—what's this that pub is called—Bartley Dunne's. Just up from that.'

'Did you ever drink in Bartley Dunne's?'

'God knows, I forget.'

Then:

'There's something I wanted to tell you—' Father? Dada? Oh God help me, God '—I think I'm homosexual.'

The snow went on falling, the tyres crunching over it, carrying us across Westmeath. My father laughed, the short bottomless laugh of resignation he gave when Noel didn't turn up for work or when *The Irish Times* criticized Fianna Fáil again. 'What can *I* do?'

'I just thought I ought to tell you.' I had said it. The words vibrated like the wipers shoving the snow left, right off the windscreen. I looked out at fieldfares darting along white hedges spattered red with haws.

'I used to feel that way,' my father spoke. 'But I was ashamed of it.'

[65]

'What?'

'I was attracted to men that way.'

Beautiful warmth spreading still. Where was it coming from?

'When was this?'

'When I was young. Your age.'

'And?'

'I was a very ... slight young man then.'

'And what did you do?'

Smile grimace shrug. It was as if the warmth was coming from him, from his sallow left hand on the wheel, from his jaw already silvering with stubble, his silver rib of hair plumed back on the dark forehead. I had a sudden longing to lean into his arms and lie there.

'... and then I married,' he was saying.

I sat up again. 'How did you feel then?'

'I found peace then.' He spoke carefully. 'It wasn't a very—kkmm!—passionate affair ... I mean, I couldn't say I was head over heels in love with ... Mama.' He stopped speaking.

The warmth faded, as if a window had been opened. Found peace then? It wasn't a very passionate affair. What did that mean? And what sort of peace was it that vanished with my mother? When, the week she went to Rome, he had turned into a trembling ghost, his hand so shaky he couldn't get the key in the door, spilling the soup as he served us dinner? Peace? He couldn't even drive to Donegal on his own.

'It's getting heavier. I think we'll stop in Mayo. We can see what it's like in the morning.'

We? Not me. I was ice cold suddenly. We were driving out of feudal Westmeath now; ahead, the roadworks slicing away a quarter-mile curve of roadside trees from Major Daly's estate. 'I don't think I will, father.'

'I beg your pardon?'

'I don't think I'll go to Donegal. I think I'll stay the night in Major Daly's.' I pointed to the gates ahead.

'If that's what you want.' His voice had turned hollow.

'I might see you up there in a few days. I can always take a bus.'

'Have you money?' His face white as the snowy verge he drew in to.

None. 'Plenty, thanks.' I took my bag from the back seat, shut the door with a slam I had not intended on his—

'I'll be praying for you.'

Tears slipping down my cheekbones, I watched the car disappear into the snowflakes. Then I walked up the avenue to the big house, a home big enough for me still to hide in, a house to hide my home in.

Bare tall beech trees, thickets of snowy bamboo below, formed a valley winding for half a mile up the slope, then down, suddenly revealing an opera scene—half County Westmeath dressed in white, Lough Owel a black backdrop to the mansion before which, framed in his ionic portico, Major Daly stood as if about to deliver a ringing aria. *Pater omnipotens.*

'And here you are …' A touch of the actor in the unsurprisable voice, and in the walk as he advanced to greet me. A natural for the part after a lifetime of ritualized behaviour; the look, handshake, turn back to the house as finished as his final consonants. The lost child, dreaming man, the peasant snob and watery artist surged after him. 'Come in, come in.'

The leopard skin in the hall, the old Irish water spaniel softly farting—everything was the same except Major Daly. A year to me had been more to him: suddenly he was an old man. The change was heightened by grandchildren's traces—bicycles in the passage, rock music blaring. His son had retired from the army, he explained, as he gathered drinking equipment and led the way into the library.

His desk had been cleared, rearranged, a vase of flowers stood on the table, a violent red real regimental drum lay on the floor. Sitting down heavy on the padded fender, taking whiskey bottle from one pocket, two tumblers from the other, he talked as before: the Black Pig's Dyke, the stoats, his morning readings

[67]

in the Bible. He stopped as a tall, big-hipped handsome woman stepped in. He tried to rise, couldn't, pushed furiously down on the fender and drove himself upright; standing to attention, he introduced his daughter-in-law.

Would I stay for dinner? I would. And could I—I gave a blurred account of my arrival there—stay the night? Of course. She left again and Major Daly returned to his favourite themes. Favourite to me too. Sheltered in this room, watched over by stuffed birds and by books as dead, looking out at the snow fall, feeling the whiskey warmth spread through me—I was safe. Safe from what? From myself. But wasn't this myself? Wasn't I interested in archaeology, animals and the Bible? But this was hopscotch conversation, skipping from one neutral spot to the next by the rules of politeness; skirting the awkward, skirting that skin and scarlet drum on the floor as we went down to dinner.

No skirting a big new photo-portrait of Queen Elizabeth II on the dining-room wall.

'We'll sit you opposite her,' Major Daly's son said, his smile half quizzical as he drew out my chair.

'Isn't that a bit ...' I faltered as his smile withdrew. I fumbled for a smooth word, '... obvious?'

'How do you mean?' Old jeans and jumper, but his Irish Guards officer voice sent my head bending down to the soup.

Silence down the table; only the sound of Major Daly's hard breathing. I looked up, continued—sounding to my own ears like a snappy terrier now—'I mean, there's a war going on a few counties away.'

'Oh we mustn't be intimidated by that.'

Intimidated by that, I returned to the hopscotch conversation his wife had begun: if the locals persisted in putting plastic wreaths on the graves she was jolly well going to let one of her gates into the churchyard to eat them.

'Let in what?' Major Daly looked up.

'Goats,' his son translated, and turned the half-quizzical smile onto his wife.

'Oh,' Major Daly said, 'I thought you said gates.'

'So did I.' I smiled.

'Then why didn't you say so?' She turned her straight smile on me.

Because your voice frightens me, you bossy West-Brit. And by the way, it's bloody bad manners, to say the least, to have a portrait of another country's head on the wall. How would you like it if you went into an English dining-room and found a portrait of de Valera—heh? 'Will goats eat plastic?' I said.

'Goats will eat anything,' Major Daly pronounced. 'Do you remember that fellow Gallard? Lived over at Coole? He kept goats. Until he had so many he called me to kill some. So I went over armed to the teeth—rifle, gun, knife. That changed his mind. He couldn't go through with it. Sent me home.'

That got us through dinner. After dinner the family faded away. Alone, Major Daly muttered to me awkwardly, 'You might give me a hand along the passage?' I understood at the toilet door what he meant, when he dropped tent-sized trousers, lowered elephant-wrinkled buttocks onto the bowl. A spatter explosion, then he made to rise, pointing angrily, ashamedly, at the roll of paper out of reach.

There, bending and wiping the landed gentry's arse, I thought of my father driving alone through the snow. What was I doing here? Avoiding him? Dodging Daddy, as Jamie said of Barrett?

Maybe but why? To be with a bigger Daddy, to be even more of a son? Shoulder supporting Major Daly's leaning hand, I went up the dark passage. At the foot of the staircase he stopped, muttered awkwardly again, 'I go upstairs rather early now …'

I wandered into the drawing-room and joined the young family. After Eights on the side table and—that other English indulgence, laughing lovingly at themselves—*To the Manor Born* on a new colour TV. The laughter was interrupted by the phone ringing. Like Peter Bowles and Penelope Keith, husband

and wife politely clashed on who should answer it. He went, returned a minute later, stood at the door and announced—voice still like Peter Bowles—'There's a bomb in the house.'

'Ohhh,' she sighed. A thousand years of civilization in the alert, bored, elongated vowel.

'He just said "There's a bomb in your house" and put down the phone.'

'You'd best ring the Garda.' She managed to mispronounce the Irish word.

He went out. She went on, 'Nothing like this has ever happened before ...'

A line of thought developed by her husband when he returned, white-faced now. 'They said not to move. They'll be here in ten minutes.' Blasé voice returning, he looked at me: 'I don't suppose you've got a bomb in your bag?'

A rush of Fenian rage to my face, followed by Croppy silence.

There was no bomb. No more conversation either. When the Guards had gone I went to bed, brilliant retorts flashing through my mind as I climbed the red-carpeted stairs. I tried one out next morning as I left, straight after breakfast: 'Thanks. It went like a bomb.'

'Haw haw haw,' said the son—three syllables of anger, confusion and disdain. He walked with me to the open door, then turned abruptly back into the house. A draught blew the door shut with a bang.

Major Daly was still in bed when I left but somehow a final, fatherly, feudal gift had found its way into my bag—a bottle of Powers Three Swallows.

I set it on my uncle Petie's kitchen table amongst the junk-shop display: sheep clippers, hammer with broken handle, jug, teapot and—a new touch—some lumps of coal. Petie wiped a smut into a smear across his nose, as if readying himself for a charade on Futility.

'Any glasses?'

He went into the scullery, wellingtons splashing on the flooded floor. Gradually he was withdrawing from all rooms to the kitchen, and in the kitchen from all corners to the hearth, where he sat on a stool against the chimney, one hand dangling over the fire; gazing at the flames as intently as his neighbours watched TV. Here he boiled his tea, his egg, smoked his pipe, drank from the bottle cellared in an old wellington, rested his back into an armchair and slept.

Here nothing changed. Maybe nothing changes anywhere, but this kitchen's outright dismissal of change, endeavour, participation, achievement always calmed me, reduced all anxieties, leaving only the elementary pulse of life, like this eternal small turf fire.

More splashing as he brought back two dripping glasses, filled them with Major Daly's whiskey, sat back on his stool, hand dangling again an inch above the flames. Here was the scene of my happy holiday childhood, so wonderful to me that once, running back from the fields, I had lain down in the moss and heather and almost fainted, overcome by delight. Now the play had moved on to another scene: my grandmother and all those other strong old black-clothed women were dead; and in each cottage now was an elderly bachelor living alone with squalor. A few sips of whiskey and my calm mood changed. Why had I come here? I wanted to be gone, out of this dump that destroyed my dream of this dump.

'Will we go into Knock?' Petie got up, set down his glass between the rusted arms of a hames. He too wanted to be out of here for a change.

'I've no car.'

'And how did you come?' Disappointed, irritated.

'Hitched.'

'You're like the fairy.'

'Have another glass.'

'I'll have it later.'

He took it for granted that the bottle was for him; as he took it for granted that my father sent him new boots, old suits, paid his ESB bill. He was a big baby, I thought. Disappointed, irritated, I poured myself another glass.

'Where are you going to? Margaret's?'

'I might.' Defiant. 'How is she?'

'I don't know.' Defiant. They spoke of each other with the absolute indifference of elderly brother and sister.

Aggressively at ease, I looked about the kitchen, took down a book from the dresser top, blew off a black inch of smuts. *The Blue Bird* by Maurice Maeterlinck. 'Whose was this?'

'Mother's.' At the holy word his voice softened.

'Father's.' Hardening again as I glanced at the knife box where a heavy silver watch and chain lay welded by rust to a bed of nails. 'Take it, I don't want it.'

'Why don't you use it?'

'It's broken. Take it. Go on, you'd better be going.' He shoved it into my hand. 'It's snowing again.'

Embarrassed, confused by anything that could not be discussed in hard dry peasant ritual style, he went to the front door and opened it. And yet that sliced-flint Western face was already quivering, tears gathering in the clouded blue eyes. 'Go on.' He shut the door after me. The tears were falling now, I knew, as the latch clicked.

Another door shut. And still I wouldn't go, was clinging to the past, the past that was clinging to me. Angry, I strolled further up, not back down the boreen, through the white mud my dream had turned to; acting absorbed in rubbing greasy rust from my grandfather's watch chain, each link stamped with a Victorian hallmark, fruit of a Lancashire coal-miner's wage. Forty years without a Christmas at home; coming back only for spring and harvest; his children born nine months after March or August. And wouldn't that—forty years ruled by their mother—help explain Petie's hair-trigger emotion, my father's, and in turn my own? Yes, now I was getting somewhere ... I stepped into the old house: threshold stone worn hollow, thatch fallen in, snow and cowdung piebalding the floor, the fire grate turned into a manger full of grey hay.

Here my father had been born in ... one two three four five six seven eight—yes, nine months after August ... in April 1910, in the first flush of peasant proprietorship. 'And you wouldn't see that'—Margaret pressing proudly thumbnail to top joint of little finger—'on the land.' That being the smallest stick, stone or weed; the land tilled, tilth raked fine with the fury of hunger, pride of possession. Turf, hay and straw ricks thatched by women, cottages lime-washed by women, gardens kept by women, children raised by women; the men in England. The see-saw tilting suddenly then—how? why?—turning all this into a desert of old men.

Walking back down the boreen littered with coal bags, bean tins, black rum bottles, I saw Petie stand at the window to watch me as far as the road. From there I looked back, saw the bare light bulb go out. Five o'clock and he was going to sleep.

I walked out to the main road and waited for a lift, passing the time polishing the old watch-case until its silver was bright as the falling snow.

− 6 −

'Morning all!' Jamie appeared at my elbow, cock-robin chest thrust out, wearing his floral tie.

'Afternoon to you,' the barman chided.

'So it is.' Jamie looked at his watch. His left arm was in white plaster.

'What'll it be?'

'Two pints, one Campari and soda.' Jamie nodded to my glass. 'Alright?'

'Alright. What happened your arm?'

'I broke it. You're a writer—have you a pen?'

Jamie made off with it to the corner where two skinhead boys vigorously signed his cast.

'Oh dear,' Jack sighed, 'Jamie's ascending again.'

As a rule anonymous-looking, Jamie's face was alive with laughter, lower lip curled out. He returned my pen, collected his drink. 'Come over and join us.'

The boys looked as if they could do with Jamie's generosity, devouring sandwiches and washing them down with the beer. Jamie did the introductions—Shay, Ger.

'What's that?' Shay nodded at the Campari.

'It's easy to lift.' Jamie steered the glass to his lips, chuckling— no other word for it—like a thrush. 'I'm not ambidextrous.'

I asked again, 'How did it happen?'

'Getting out of a taxi.'

'At forty miles an hour,' Ger said.

'We were in the country, weren't we,' Shay said, 'the fucking country.'

'Now now.' Jamie was his other, polite self again. 'Adrian's from the country.'

I said I was from the city, and Jamie said, 'I beg your pardon. What part?'

'Rathmines.'

'Same here.'

'What part?'

'Palmerston Road. Very high-haired.'

'Did you know the O'Haras?'

'They lived next door.'

Everyone has snapshots of childhood, small random pictures we instinctively hold on to, as if they sum up the past. One of mine appeared now: Jamie standing at the 12 bus stop, oiled cow-lick, pale raincoat, pale face; a cold wind cutting up Palmerston Road between the big red-brick tea-caddy houses; the fur-coated old women from the McGeogh Home in a dutiful Protestant queue; Jamie always apart. The Jamie sitting opposite me was so like the snapshot Jamie, it was hard to believe I hadn't put the two together before.

The neat pattern was broken as he got up suddenly, went to the door to watch a horse and cart rattle by. 'A horse! A horse!' He vanished into the street.

'Same again?' Shay stood up, took money from the heap on the table. Some quibbling about his age brought Ger up to the counter too. I was alone when Jamie returned, carrying in his good, cupped hand some golden balls of horse-droppings, still steaming, and placed them on the table amongst the money. 'My kingdom for a horse.'

'That'll do,' the barman said, serene, firm, as if bringing an audition to a close.

'I remember you now,' I said.

'Really?' Jamie wiped his hand clean. Face rosy with excitement, his fifties quiff undone, he turned to the boys returning refused from the counter. 'Will we ride on? I'm due back in the hospital—'

'We'll wait for you in Bartley's.'

'Vamos, chicos!' Chuckling, jostling them before them, calling back to me, 'Might see you down there this evening? I'm off duty at five,' Jamie went out the door.

'God help the patients.' The barman attended to the horse-droppings. 'God help the patients.'

'He'll be the next one,' some happy voice said.

Colin: 'Again.'

'Well I'm not visiting him this time,' Jack complained from the corner. 'I've had enough dragging up to St Pat's.'

Colin: 'Aw. And he went up to see you.'

No matter. Work. Work.

Through the library's curved-glass roof the seagulls' feet were stranded goldfish flapping high overhead. The door swung open, Laurence stepped in, stood before a hundred upturned faces, announced—'Admirable people ... IN YOUR OWN WAY!'—and stepped out again. My stomach knotted. And he had once had a play in the Abbey, sweet applause ... and then? Pit-pat. The gulls flapped about above. Pt-pt. My pen scratched across the paper.

The plot was so simple. The hero arrived in Dublin, blank, passive, pure, still as a glass of water. He drifted about, tinged by each incident, each encounter. And then—the next step was so blindingly obvious I couldn't believe no other writer had thought of it.

—What's this it is again?

—Everything just ... comes to a point.

—Yes, but how exactly?

—It's like when you put an electric current into water—

—But doesn't that ... kill you?

—You know what I mean. Everything's the same, but ... transformed.

Turning into Duke Street I saw my brother Kevin hand in hand with Celia. First reaction: to duck into the Bailey, until I saw that they were going into the Bailey—when I followed them inside, walked to the bar, ordered, turned, looked surprised at seeing them sitting on the end banquette.

Kevin's teeth were shining, white against a sun-tanned face; an open smile as he saw me. He was back from Italy where he had been buying shoes for the family business. Celia was holding his brown hand. It had been their first time apart since their wedding, that wedding which had cracked our family shell; which had felt like summer holidays in Connemara long ago, when we had walked into the combers, falling green walls breaking white on top of us, smothering us, throwing us back laughing deafened onto Renvyle strand. Our father, like a periwinkle bent-pinned out of his shell, listening wriggling to Celia's father commend the Irish navvies and tattie-hokers in Scotland; refusing the offer of a large cigarillo, a wee Teachers; our mother pale-rigid as Celia's mother's blue-rinsed hair; our sister smiling nervously as Celia's brother laid a hand on her knee and explained the second-hand car trade. Again, again, we had run into these breakers regardless. Kevin had done it: Kevin the no-egg eater, Kevin not interested in Mayo, Kevin only twenty-five, had broken out, and the sea was pouring in.

'What'll you have?' His hand went down into his hip pocket. Even in that, I noticed, he resembled our father.

I turned to show off, called the barman by name—and saw Stephen stroll in, arm in arm with Helen.

'So—' Unwinding the white silk scarf, he sat down slowly. 'What's all this?'

[77]

I introduced them. Helen smiled wanly—'No sign of Jonathan?'

'No sign.'

'What'll you have, Stephen?' Again my brother's hand went
down, bringing up Irish and Italian money.

'Who's been on holiday then?' Stephen smiled.

'Work, as a matter of fact.' Celia's tone—amusement and
toughness combined—reminded me of the careful, sharp chords
she played on our piano. Kevin—as he had that evening Celia
refused the egg mayonnaise—turned to her and again, as if
catching the tonic note, turned back to Stephen, said, 'Very
matter-of-fact work.'

'Shoes?' Stephen raised his eyebrows.

'What do you do?' Celia enquired, mother hen outspreading
wings.

'I do penance.'

'Where?'

'Everywhere.'

Celia persisted easily, like an adult, one hand held behind
her back, boxing playfully with a child. 'Who pays you?'

'A leading Irish newspaper, as they say.'

'So you're a journalist.' Celia translated flatly.

'Hi, guys!'

Only then Helen looked up, as Jonathan arrived: six-foot
handsome, baggy London-fashion clothes, unconvincing Irish
accent, sitting down oblivious on the end of Stephen's white
silk scarf, turning to put an arm about Helen, kissing her cheek,
murmuring something, drawing a lover's cloak of privacy about
them.

Slowly Stephen stood up—pinned scarf slipping from his
neck like a bandage—and strolled to the toilet, or, as he said,
lavatory. Kevin glanced at his watch, turned to Celia. 'What
time are we expected for dinner?'

'What's the hurry?'

I could see she wanted more of my brother's company.

Kevin—working all day with his father, having morning coffee and lunch with him, dropping in to see him on the way home from work each evening—would be reporting this evening on his Italian dealings, leaving Celia yet again to chat with my mother, to be dragged by the heels like Hector behind Mama's chariot of small-talk, around and around the citadel of her power.

She frowned, rose reluctantly as Kevin finished his drink; Helen, Jonathan hardly lifting eyes from one another to nod goodbye.

'I'll be with you.' I walked with them to the door.

Hand in hand they went up Duke Street—and I turned suddenly down to Bartley Dunne's, only then remembered that Stephen was still in the toilet, that I had done to him as he had once done to me.

Mock Georgian window-panes curtained by pink satin, and old theatre bills—*The Dog Beneath the Skin ... Desire Under the Elms*; the doorpanes covered by old photos—Sybil Thorndike's classic profile averted as I pushed inside through solid fear.

Pitch dark at first, then, by candle and red-shaded lamplight, people appeared. A sleek black-haired barman, handsome in a white duck jacket, took my order with a glaze of indifference. I sat at the counter. Two English voices alongside—

'So we went back to the Burlington, up to my room. He'd got the idear—'

'You staying there? What's it like?'

'Good. Good parking facilities.'

'You could almost be in the UK, couldn't you.'

'Well, I wouldn't go that far. So I got his trousers down ...'

So here I was in the thick of it, in Bartley Dunne's, antechamber to the underworld.

—What in the name of God are you doing here?

—Waiting for Jamie.

—But this is ridiculous, Adrian. Think back to your boyhood. All those nights you lay awake dreaming of what you'd do when you were twenty-one. First plane to Cairo. Straight to a red-light nightclub crammed with naked women, where you'd stay till you were at least forty. And here you are in a Dublin bar for homosexual men. What happened?

—I don't know what to say to that.

—And when will you know?

—When I've tried it. Oh God, why is my stomach in knots?

—Queer fear.

—You don't have that with Jamie.

—I know him.

—You mean you've placed him in your cautious peasant's graph-book. He's from Palmerston Road, family neighbour, next door to O'Hara, to Niamh Barrett—so you're … at home with him. Mm, this is very interesting. You don't think of Jamie as queer at all, do you? Queer for you means fear.

—We could sit here all night talking. I came here to do something about it. I'm going to have a look around.

'There you are.'

'Jamie—'

Plaster-cast garlanded with autographs now, Jamie was sitting by the back wall in a crowd of boys, his oatmeal sportscoat hanging off one shoulder, short back and sides head leaning in over the centre of the table to catch what one of the boys was saying. He sat back laughing, threw a 'Still there?' glance at me, then leaned forward again—'Do you know Pier Paolo Pasolini?'

'Are they Italians?' A boy rolled up his sleeves, bared leg-sized arms shining gold.

Jamie threw another high laugh up at the smoke cloud, caught sight of me again, still lingering on the threshold, and, ignoring me completely now, leaned further into the close circle of young shoulders.

Coward, mouse ... Calling myself more names, I wandered out into the dark, welcoming the punishing cold; and up South King Street where I ran into Stephen as he wandered up Grafton Street, head down, elbows deep in Helen's gabardine coat pockets. 'Where are Helen and Jon?'

'Up there.' Stephen pointed to Jonathan's flat, high above Rice's bar. The bedroom window was lighted. 'She's moved in with him.'

'Good view from up there.' I rubbed it in. 'I had a drink with him the other night. You can see right across the Green.'

'Where did you get to?'

I told him.

'You're such a fucking idiot.'

'Eejit, please. And who cares if it's "toilet" or "lavatory". How can someone as intelligent as you be bothered with such ... *specks* of snobbery. It's incredible.'

'What the hell are you doing down in Bartley Dunne's? You're not queer. Why don't you screw a few women?'

'And be happy like you? I told you. I—'

'It's normal. Happens to everyone sometime.'

'Does it?'

'Christ, do I have to teach you everything?'

'Christ, it's freezing.'

'Is it?'

'Give us your coat. In fact, give us it anyway. What the hell do you wear Helen's coat for?'

'Here.' Grimacing as if peeling off a skin, Stephen took off the grey schoolgirl's gabardine. 'Keep it.'

'There are other girls besides Helen.'

'You wouldn't understand.'

'Stephen, why do you always talk down to me?'

'Because I've no confidence. None.' He was drunk. We stopped at the top of Kildare Street, looked down. There was a small crowd lit up by police-car flashes, a TV crew's lamps.

'What's happening?'

'Offenses Against the State Bill. Second Stage. Come on.'

Stephen was acting the boss again. His press card, family connections, drunk confidence took us through the gates and into the House. The bar was packed with members, relations, friends, journalists—three deep at the counter. No chance of a drink. Stephen lit a joint, continued talking. 'No confidence. None. Ever. That's why I talk the way I do. That's why I—'

'I think that's why I—'

'*Ssshh!* We're in the fucking Dáil.' He passed me the joint. '*Ejaculatio praecox*—it's the commonest thing.'

'And does it ever happen to you? I mean, when you're in bed with all those—'

'For Christ's sake! Come on, we'll go up to the Chamber ...'

Already the crowd was moving upstairs to the visitors' gallery. Faces familiar from newspapers pushed their way down the passage. The air was tight with excitement. Mary Cole's father, a senator now, hat shoved down almost over his eyes, coat open, stumbled past, drunk. A TD, his face bloated with drink, blank with disillusion, came out of a cloakroom, buttoning his fly, saying, 'Now it's happening, now it's happening.'

'What?'

'Where have you been?'

'Enjoying ourselves,' Stephen said. 'Why?'

'Well, there's been a bomb attack.'

'Better put out that joint.'

The Chamber was crowded, the debate blazing.

'The Deputy is talking nonsense and it is typical of him. It runs in the family like a wooden leg ...'

'Did I tell you that Helen has moved in with Jonathan?'

'You did.'

'Did I say that they're going to live in London?'

'Good. You can forget about her now.'

'I *can't* ...' Stephen looked as if he might cry. He turned away to the debate again. His mother's face looked up at him from the Opposition benches.

'I said you were facing two ways.'

'On a point of order.'

'Sit down.'

'Is the House aware that two people have lost their lives and forty people have been injured in O'Connell Street?'

'That is not a point of order. I have told the Deputy to sit down ...'

The facts seeped in. We sat silent, looking down into the Chamber. There was a far-away flat heavy bang—another explosion. Then a silence as loud. A porter entered the Chamber with a water carafe, handed it to a front-bench member, who tipped a measure into the tumbler before him, sipped deeply.

'Neat idea.'

'He has to do without the tonic though.'

'Well, there's a war on ...'

'You did worse than that. You tried it on my father, and he was a Sinn Féin member in the Tan days. He wasn't an opportunist like a lot of them nowadays ...'

'About this—'

'Will you relax —it's nothing.'

'Nothing? How would you like it if I said Helen is nothing?'

'Jesus—I'm going.'

'Can I stay in your place?'

'What's wrong with the Brazen Head?'

'I'm leaving that.'

'There's Helen's bed, if you want it.'

Someone hissed 'Sssh!'

'We meet here in the House tonight under dark clouds. Explosions are taking place here in our city. Citizens of the twenty-six counties are being killed. We offer our deepest sympathy to the relatives of those people ...'

'OK.'

'Are you for or against?'

'I have tried to get the government to take action over the past three years ...'

'Are you for or against?'

'Come on.' Stephen stood up. 'Let's go.'

Walking across the forecourt under the plane trees, their fallen seedballs crackling underfoot, I felt the same flutter of anticipation I had felt leaving Major Daly's gate-lodge. The big gates were opened, latched, locked behind us.

'Will we look into Power's?'

Knots of people were wandering down the street to the hotel. Stephen shook his head. In the yellow street-light his face seemed old. His voice was husky. 'I just want to go home.'

ESTHER

− 7 −

If I think of then, I think of Esther. Not that she stands out. I forget how we met. Because she doesn't stand out, she seems all the more part of that time when everything—work, family, solitary walks, pubs—was a tangle from which we were each spinning our own thread.

I remember our first date—if you can call arranging to meet in The Castle a date.

Wandering around the Green, passing the time beforehand, I saw Fr Treston, an old teacher from school. As usual when figures from the past appeared, I thought of making a run for it. As usual I didn't.

'Hello, Father.' My accent improving.

'Ah, Adrian.' He resumed looking through the railings. 'Wasn't there a statue here?' He spoke as if it were days, not years, since we had met.

'Was there?'

He was the same as ever. Schoolboy face, black raincoat faded greenish, much-mended shoes.

'A Lord Eglinton, wasn't it?'

'That's right.' I remembered then. 'It was blown up. That's a while ago.'

'The first I heard of it.' He raised his gaze from the fresh grass patch. 'And what are you doing with yourself?'

He too was walking about the Green. I walked alongside, talking of book reviews and English-language teaching. Fr Treston listened in calm silence. I looked about for some other topic. The College of Surgeons appeared. I pulled a rabbit from the hat.

'Is that Aesculapius?'

'Ah ...' Fr Treston smiled up at the statue. It reminded me of school, reading Tacitus, when at the one-line mention of Ireland Fr Treston looked up from the page and smiled a similar 'Ah ...', wistful that the Romans hadn't made more effort and brought us into the happy sunlit Mediterranean world of his imagination.

'Why does he always have a snake around his staff?'

'It seems to have been part of his cult.' Fr Treston made a shudder. 'One reason it didn't catch on in Ireland.'

'They say that the story of St Patrick banishing snakes symbolized his banishing the old pagan life.'

'Really?' More calm silence. I rattled on.

'Isn't it interesting that snakes were a symbol of life in the pagan world, but Christianity shows them as a symbol of evil?'

End of calm silence. 'No. It shows their fulfilment.'

'How do you mean?' It came out sounding abrupt. I smiled, tacked on a 'Father'.

'In Christ.' Fr Treston spoke shortly, as at school when I had made a silly mistake. 'John tells us that "As Moses lifted up the serpent in the wilderness, even so must the Son of Man be lifted up ..."'

As he spoke, it seemed as if it really were only days since I had seen him. He was, unlike Lord Eglinton's statue, a monument still standing to another world. While I over the past couple of years had drunk with Stephen, Jamie, Percy, tried to write and make love, Fr Treston had been living as ever: saying 7 a.m. Mass in that late Georgian mansion, teaching Greek and

Latin, taking evening strolls like this, sorties out of camp. I had a sudden desire to establish some other, adult intimacy or agreement with that ordered world. But already Fr Treston was moving off, looking at his watch as he had in class when the bell rang, asking after my parents—and then he was gone through the crowd, his stiff-backed anonymous figure drawing glances of unconcern from people who reminded me suddenly of myself.

People who took charge of their own lives? Individuals free from the family church world? That was rich. I went over our conversation as I wandered into the Green. What had I wanted to say? That I disagreed, wasn't so sure. Why hadn't I? Because I wasn't so sure ...

As usual, as all paths in the Green converged at the centre flowerbed, that set me thinking about my novel. To write, you had to have a point of view. What was mine? My family had been peasants since the Bronze Age or whenever peasants began; I was a Catholic, educated by Jesuits to regard the individual will with infinite suspicion. Not much of a base to view from. I skirted the bronze bullrush fountain. Or did a point of view need to be elevated, like Lord Eglinton on his plinth, Aesculapius on his pediment? More important, did I believe in individual points of view at all? I crossed the playing-field patterned with people—lying, sitting, single, in pairs. But how else could you view the sublime generality of life? Wandering out of the Green, I packed my thoughts away again—like my mother when she tried to sort out her handbag, like Percy when he tried to edit his journal but hadn't been able to throw a single thing away.

A face glimpsed from the train, a fox caught in car headlights can come back to us hours or days later, and we picture them about their business. In the bar that evening Fr Treston's face appeared, a genie from the Guinness bottle before me, and I wondered what was he up to now, 9.30 p.m.? Watching TV was unlikely. Reading? Reading what? A novel was hard to imagine. His old pal Pausanias? In the way St Ignatius bade us picture Christ's passion, I tried to give substance to this vision of Fr Treston. Bare room. Iron single bed. Crucifix on wall. Grizzled head bent over an account of a Greek pagan temple. I was picturing his forehead furrow in the lamplight, when—

'Hi!' Esther appeared by my side.

Not so beautiful or brainy to make waiting for her unnerving, but now that she had appeared I wanted to run from this physical presence. She took my empty bottle, put it on the counter, ordered another—her American voice turning 'By the neck' into a vivid expression. At our last meeting, seeing me nod to someone down the bar, she had said, 'You know him?'

'Gerry? He's an artist.'

'He is in bed.' Adding mysteriously, 'I recommend him.'

'Hear this—' She sat beside me now, sipped her pint, licked clean her full upper lip '—I was coming down Leeson Street ...'

Not beautiful maybe, but noticeable. Not just her accent; her slow sleepy movement too, and her dark ringed eyes. From the next table, through his court circle of boys, Bibby's sandy-lashed eyes stare-glared at me.

'... and this guy was following me. So I stopped. And he said'— she mimicked cruelly a broken-backed Irish accent—"Would you like to sleep with me?" Jesus, he must have been fifty.'

'What did you say?'

'I felt so sorry for him, I just said, "I'm going to meet my boyfriend."'

My cock sat up.

'And do you know what he said then?' Esther took another long sip. 'Christ, the number of stark-staring mad people walking loose around this town—he said, "I don't suppose you know anyone who would?"'

Each time we met she had a story. It seemed she only had to step out the door for propositions to rain down on her. She was

like the obscure-seeming curio shop which everyone thinks he alone has found, where bargains come easy.

That was the exciting part, the frightening part too; more so tonight as Esther felt in her bag for tobacco and papers, came across a tab of contraceptive pills, pressed one into her palm and washed it down with the last of her Guinness. She rolled a cigarette, said, 'Will we push off?'

'Where?'

She shrugged and stood up, strolled to the Ladies. I pressed my shoes to the floor to stop my knees from shaking.

'What on earth'—Bibby, barrister-at-law and advocate of Dionysian excess, turned to me—'are you doing with that ridiculous girl?'

'She's a friend.'

Bibby smiled, pressed on like a Legionary of Mary asking if you still went to Mass. 'You're still living with Stephen?'

I shook my head. 'He has a new girlfriend.'

'Poontang,' one of the boys said.

'Ah yes.' Bibby smiled again. 'Poontang.'

'What's poontang?'

Esther explained as we walked out to Ranelagh, went on to talk of some poems she had published and of her waitressing work. I spoke on the Irish short story and the job I had got with Contract Cleaners. That took us to my new flat, my father's latest present.

'You own all this?' She paused in taking off her jacket.

'For a year.' I played down the size, led her to the sitting-room. But in the kitchen opening the bottle we had bought, I heard her go back down the passage—'Jesus'—opening doors—'H'—shutting them—'Christ.'

A staid place with compulsory venetian blinds. Through the slats I saw the sallow-faced girl who walked past beneath the street-lamp every evening. The retired couple were already

asleep downstairs. Upstairs the newly married couple were busy in bed, the headboard banging against the wall.

'I go mad when that happens—when I'm alone.' Esther looked at the ceiling. 'What do you do?'

'Listen. What do you?

'Bite the pillow.'

We kissed then.

It was sweet to sit on the carpet by the fire, to drink and talk as we undressed each other. Esther was a big girl: when her camisole came off, her breasts hit her middle with soft slaps. Like a connoiseur of pleasure she paused, put down her glass, reached a book from a shelf and read aloud—

'But there is neither East nor West, Border, nor breed nor birth,
When two strong men stand face to face, though they come from the
    ends of the earth.'

'Major Daly—this old man I knew—he used to quote that all the time. He told me that once when he was in the Hindu Kush—'

She drew off her jeans.

I took the book, like another gourmet prolonging pleasurable anticipation—

'I went into a public-'ouse to get a pint o' beer,
The publican 'e up an' sez, "We serve no red-coats here."
The girls be'ind the bar they laughed an' giggled fit to die,
I outs into the street again an' to myself sez I:
  O it's Tommy this, an' Tommy that, an' "Tommy, go away";
  But it's "Thank you, Mister Atkins," when the band begins to play—'

'Let's go to bed.' Esther got up.

'The band begins to play, my boys, the band begins to play,
  Oh it's "Thank you, Mister Atkins," when the band begins to play.'

Esther plucked the book from my hand, put it back on the shelf. Playing was over. I followed her broad back into the bedroom. A minute's reprieve as she stood to admire a teacup on the dressing-table.

'It's Sèvres.'

'Dinky.' She drew a fingertip down a cherub's blushing downcast cheek. 'What's the L stand for?'

'King Louis.' I outlined its provenance: the King of France, my Aunt Rita, me.

Me facing the music now. My flute standing rigid, playing yet again—as Esther drew it into her—its short sudden note.

'Aw, shoot!' she laughed.

Nothing to her, it seemed; everything to me. Lying on her side, hand under cheek, her big tiny-nippled breasts tumbled together bright against her brown arms, she suggested twists she enjoyed: my finger, my tongue, her hand, her mouth. That I enjoyed too. But she understood. I was on fire for the one simple thing. She seemed to take it as a challenge, or an amusement maybe. One night she arrived at the door, drew a white silk nightdress out of her pocket—the long gentle approach. In Oakley Road another night she drew me into a garden, up against a tree—the sudden attack. The same outcome—

'Aw, shoot!'

'Experience is the basis of art, but is not itself art. Art is like a tree, drawing up experience through its roots and turning it into a natural yet heavenly shape: leaves and branches forming a pure parabola. The human equivalent of this is culture; without it the elements remained scattered, earthbound facts ...'

The doorbell rang, I dropped my pencil, ran tiptoe to the window, looking down just as my father looked up. God! I shoved my thoughts on the novel into the drawer, pressed the buzzer.

'Yes ... I was just passing ... I thought I'd look in for a minute ...' He followed me inside, furtively tossed a present—a pair of black morocco leather slippers—behind the door, sitting down then in the best chair, taking off his hat. A red tomato sun, sliced by the venetian blinds, fell upon his bare head. 'Well, how's the writing going?'

'OK—will you have tea?'

'No thanks.'

'It's nice. Assam. I got this ...' I showed him the caddy, red and black-lacquered.

'*Oh* ... I'd like that.' That look again, like a boy shown a gift out of reach. That other look then as he glanced down, murmured, 'Are they the only shoes you have?'

Twenty-six, but still deep in jungle warfare for independence: with the instinctive accuracy of the pigmy spear-thrower, I had bought this pair of wrecked Oxfam brogues. 'They're comfortable.' I tried out a direct look. 'No news?'

He looked at me, the five-foot-six-inch thorn in his side. 'We're having the staff dance in the Clarence this year. Come along if you've nothing better to do.'

No thanks. 'Thanks.'

Anything he liked, he liked more of. He poured a second cup of Assam, drank it in one thirsty gulp. 'Hugh Bennett's retiring.'

'How is he?'

'Well, I was just looking at him there this morning. The same bloody old anorak on him this twenty years. You'd swear he hadn't a tosser.' The slang meant he was nervous.

'Will Noel run that business now?'

'Ah yes ...' He stopped short as the doorbell rang again and his expression changed, shutting like the venetian blinds when the cord was pulled; the family face vanished, the face for the outside world appeared.

Esther? One day she had undressed on the way up the stairs, jumped in the door near-naked. With relief I saw Stephen on the step. He was lonely lately, often wandering out from Leeson Street to visit.

'A glass of whine?' He set a bottle on the hall table.

'Whine not.'

Awkwardly my father stood up, the sliced-tomato sunset sliding down his face. 'I'll be off.'

'Stephen, this is my father.'

'Mr Kenny—Hello.'

One reason we are fascinated when we catch someone unawares—the face glimpsed from the train, the fox in the headlights—is that we expect to learn something from such unselfconscious naturalness. Seeing my father in strange company gave me that sort of excited curiosity. With others he was no longer my father but a strange simple man.

'I was telling you about Stephen,' I yoked them together, 'You said you knew his father, he was a TD for Fianna Fáil.'

'The most corrupt party in Western Europe.' Like the fox into shadows, Stephen vanished behind his cynicism, peeped out again as my father, moving from one foot to the other, went on—

'That's right.' And then, 'Well, I knew your uncle better. Is he still up there in Thomas Street?'

'Frank?' Stephen emerged slowly.

Shyly my father chafed his hands. I felt no sympathy. The unease came from his way of life: family and business, the boss in both; twin tracks of one railway line, off of which he was lost. As if eager to learn, or to remember, he sat down again, listening as Stephen talked to me about—what else?—Helen. She and Jonathan were living in London. He had been over to visit them.

'Where in London?'

'Holland Park.'

My father nodded. 'That's on the Central Line?'

Who was this man going on about London?—who only a few years before had told us at home how, killing time in Hyde Park, he had met a woman who had sat down beside him and asked him if he fancied going to the cinema—

'And what did you say?' My mother stiffened as if transfixed by a javelin.

'I said—kkm!—that I had to go to Confession.'

'Well, that was the very thing to say! That was God trying you.'

'Do you know London well, Mr Kenny?' Like many another gently reared, Stephen was respectful before what he felt must be a tougher type.

'Only to go over for the Shoe Fair, in Olympia.'

'That's Earls Court?'

'That's right. That's my beat. My God, what a city.' My father breathed out in awe. 'No wonder they don't care about us. Sure why would they?' He took his hat, moved for the door. I followed, slipped him the Assam tea caddy, searched for a sentence to seal a meeting that had gone well.

'I might see you at the staff dance.'

'Please yourself.' He smiled.

'He's nice' Stephen said. 'Tough.'

Tough? 'I know,' I said.

'You don't know how lucky you are.'

'Don't you start.' For me Stephen was the lucky one. 'How are you getting on with Sheila?'

'That dopehead? Do you know what she came out with the other night? That she'd like to grow antlers and go to live in Lapland ...'

Together we trailed into town, ended up in Rice's seedy bar. Mud-coloured carpet, aero-board ceiling, net curtain sagging like a giant string vest. As always, Stephen knew someone.

'Donald. What happened?'

I took in the black blue yellow puffed eye, blood-crusted nostrils; caught bits of the story—drunk ... docks ... docker. Under the table my knees knocked. This was what was in store for me. This, the absolute, had to be gone through before I was free. From what? Why?

'Was this Before or After?' No-father, many-lovers Stephen smiled.

'Do you know what he said?' Donald pit-patted his swollen cheek. '"Give me a frock," he said, "and I'll do anything!" My God, I thought—Heaven. And then—'

'No modelling for you for a while.'

'And when I finally did untie myself and stumbled out into the rosy-fingered dawn,' Donald stroked a red-ringed wrist, 'what did I see across the street? Remember the ad I did for Smithwicks? A twenty-foot photo of myself on a hoarding.' He mimed his poster face's manly grin poised over a frothy pint.

Through a thrill of horror I mimed an answering grin. *What was I doing here?* Ice cubes dissolving in an abandoned lager. Half an egg sandwich ripening on the window-ledge. Through the grey net curtain I saw Jamie cross the street, cock-robin chest thrust out.

'Evening all.' He sauntered in. Arm mended. *Irish Times* baton in hand. 'Fruit juice, please.' He addressed the lounge boy in his doctor's voice. 'And a packet of peanuts.' Calm.

'Nice to unwind.' Drew a stethoscope from his pocket, a packet of Sweet Afton from its coils, unrolled his newspaper.

Silence. Donald picking at dried blood grains. Stephen blowing smoke rings—his mind miles away, his face full of longing.

'Fruit and nuts,' Jamie intoned.

Donald smiled. Winced again.

Stephen didn't raise his gaze from the smoke ring, a halo wriggling to the ceiling, as if following it in his mind up through the aero-board holes, up up up through three floors to the flat where Helen and Jonathan had made love; from where Jonathan had run to do her bidding, fetching late-night cigarettes or wine, one night climbing over the railings into the

Green, coming back with a sheaf of tulips from that centre flowerbed; from where they had gone to London.

'God, it's dead here.' Jamie stood up.

So did I. Any excuse to escape. Together we turned down South King Street. 'Which way are you going?'

Jamie yawned as we passed Bartley Dunne's. 'Not there anyway.'

'And where?' I flexed my chest.

'Home for a cup of tea?'

This simple directness gave Jamie authority. Nothing to do with his voice, plain as his oatmeal sportscoat; yet everything to do with his voice. Through its plain glass the message was clear: I do as I like. Come along if you like.

'Alright.'

We walked up Stephen Street, past the house my father had wanted to buy for me; a Sold sign hung over the eighteenth-century doorframe of rusticated granite.

'She's nice'—Jamie glanced at a passing girl. 'Did you see her skirt? I noticed one like that last week, and this week every girl in town has one. They must be watching all the time.'

'Like you.'

Jamie smiled.

'You like girls, Jamie?'

'Ah yeh.'

'Ever sleep with one?'

'A couple. But I love boys. I'm a very simple person.'

'You're a very nice person. Most of the time.'

'Always the proviso.' Jamie did his chuckle. 'Here's a Twelve.' He held out his mended arm before a bus. 'Are you gay?'

'I don't know.'

'Good answer that.' He ran an eye over the conductor. 'Palmerston Road, please.'

The lime trees breathed fresh air into the dark; fresh not only because the day's traffic was done, but because my traffic here was slowly—so slowly—winding down; each link broken releasing a little more oxygen. O'Hara's house had been sold; at the gate now watching a lap-dog foul the footpath, a stranger stood savouring a cigar, glancing at me blankly as I passed by, a blank look too for Jamie.

His father had died, his mother had sold their house and moved to a smaller one. We went up Cowper Road, past my parents' house, rose lamplight glowing behind their curtained bedroom window. My insides rippled like cellophane before heat as I went by.

'Your father,' Jamie glanced incuriously in the gate, 'he wears a hat, doesn't he?'

'That's right.' Stomach relaxing again as we turned the corner. 'Didn't yours too?'

'Em …' The hesitation bringing more fresh air, 'Yeh.' Still more air flowing through his random chat, a snorkel to the surface from my clan world. 'Do you think Barrett's poetry is any good.'

'I do.'

Jamie pushed open a tiny tinny gate. 'Here we are.' Same tone of voice—'I got him into bed once.'

'Barrett?'

'He jumped out again'—Jamie turned the doorkey—'and got sick ' Looked into a small sitting-room where a grey-haired woman sat before a colour TV—'It's only me.' And still the same tone of voice, fascinating, like listening to a singer ascend a terraced crescendo. Pointed politely upstairs, switched on a landing light—'Would you like to …?'

From the bathroom window I could see across back gardens the back of my parents' house, my old bedroom window dark. Over there—Home. Here—Jamie's home. There—a place apart. Here—a place that was part of Jamie's life. From here he set out to work, to Mass, or to drink and chase boys; here he returned with his stethoscope, or a broken arm. As soon spring

[99]

from this window across a hundred yards of glass-topped walls and apple trees onto my old windowsill as join my sacred home with my life.

Silver sugar bowl on formica table. Fresh air too in the thinned-down family furniture.

'Jamie, what did your father do?'

'Doctor. How many spoons?'

'One. And your grandfather?'

'He had a pub down the country. Why?'

'I'm trying to explain your assurance.'

'But I'm chicken-livered.'

'How can you say that?'

Jamie didn't answer. Assurance. He looked about the kitchen, found the biscuit box. Only forty, but already the lines across his forehead were being squared by vertical ones. Odd as two left shoes: as likely to pick up a boy in a bar as a copy of *L'Osservatore Romano* in a church—or both; as likely to be wrong as right, Jamie was like anyone else—but with the clear ring you get when you tap a fingernail on glass crystal. Natural in the effortless way someone with a good eye connects with a ball, he had the gift which somehow makes the odd shoes into a matching pair.

The stairs creaked as his mother went up to bed. Jamie dipped a fig roll in his tea, intoned dryly, 'Home sweet home.'

'Have you ever lived away?'

'Whenever I could.'

'Why not now?'

'No dough. Who'd give me a job?'

'I think you're the best doctor I know.'

'So would you believe me if I said you're not gay?' Jamie sucked the biscuit. 'Well, no more than's good for you.'

'Always the proviso.'

Jamie smiled. 'You're just afraid of it. Everyone's afraid of something.'

'What are you afraid of?'

'Let's not get personal.' He did another chuckle.

Fresh air. Not getting personal, chatting with a cocksucker not about that but about people, writers, painters; Jamie's remarks as plain refreshing as the tea.

'Did you know Van Gogh painted five sunflowers?'

'Five pictures?'

'So I read in the paper.' He took out his cigarettes. 'I wonder why only one of them is famous?'

'I don't know.'

'I don't either.' Emptied his pockets in a search for matches.

Looking at his stethoscope tangled about the newspaper baton, I thought of Aesculapius and his snake, of my conversation with Fr Treston, of Bibby's evangelical zeal. I lived by omens, stepping-stones of superstition. There were more ways than one across the river, I thought.

'Still writing?' He set the teapot to stew on the stove.

'Ever try it yourself?'

'All the time.'

'What?'

'Poetry.' Stooping, lighting a Sweet Afton from the gas-flame. 'I'm not sure if I'm a poet, though.'

'Would you like to be?'

'More than anything.'

'Really? Maybe you are.'

'I don't know.'

'Good answer that.'

Jamie laughed. Then, shyly—'Would you like to hear one?'

Somehow the table had turned, now I seemed to be in charge. He went upstairs, returned with a school exercise book and read aloud, fidget fingers twisting a thread loose from his cuff.

'*Do boys want to be made love to by their father*

And is he tenderest when he weeps ...?' Jamie looked up—'Are you sure I'm not keeping you?'

He spoke even his poetry in that same plain conversational

tone. It took me a minute to realize the last line was addressed to me.

'Not at all. I can spend the night around the corner.' As I said it, I felt home and life shuffle an inch closer together.

− 8 −

If I think of then, I think of mornings too—the see-saw waking moment working out where I was. Not Stephen's couch, not the venetian-blind light of my flat. White-fringed bedspread … the back of Jamie's house above back-garden apple trees. I was home. From the next room—breakfast smells, the murmur of radio news and my parents' voices. What did they have to say to each other after thirty years?

'… A young fellow, marvellous accent.' Clink of china as my father carried his tray downstairs. 'So I gave him a lift, and as soon as he got into the car I got the smell of drink off him. Nine o'clock in the morning—'

'Ah. That's enough.' Clink as my mother followed.

'And then when I dropped him off at Stillorgan, he asked me for the price of a cup of tea. So I gave him a pound note— That'll buy you a cup of tea, I said, And a great many cups of tea—*if it's tea you want*.' Click! as my father unlocked the break-fast-room door.

'Of course they get that cheap wine, God help them—' Answering click as my mother unlocked the dining-room door.

'Do we want anything for dinner?' Click! of study door key. Rustle of pull-ups, rattle of golf sticks.

'Aren't we going to the Clarence?'

'Sure that's right ...'

No goodbyes. Hall door slam.

From a front window I watched him to his car. Golf bag into boot, briefcase on passenger seat, missal on dashboard. Mass in Whitefriar Street, business till lunch, and then golf, bath, TV, bed. A spark of old fire as he looked across the road at some building workers, then at his watch, commenting on their morning tea and Milkchoc Goldgrain with a toot of his horn; drowning their chorus reply—'Fucking old bollocks!'—in his engine roar.

Silence downstairs. I tiptoed back to my bedroom, looked out and saw my mother in the garden. Not a garden of playful wildness like those on either side, ours was a peasant garden still where deeply distrusted nature was staked, stapled, wired to walls, cut back ruthlessly. But looking at my mother standing on the close-shaven lawn—likely at any moment to stoop and rip up fistfuls of Aubretia approaching the path, and yet not; simply standing there ... five minutes ... ten; praying? thinking? thinking of what? fingers touching back her tinted hair—I caught a sense of peace, light as scent. She ducked into the wash-house as Mrs Hanna appeared in the garden next door.

Dither-dither, and then I made my bed, smoothing the white cover, leaving no sign that I had spent the night there, went downstairs tiptoe and let myself out the front door; yet again left inviolate that sacred home.

Who had raised such a tumulus on this ordinary spot? My father? My mother? Both. Leaving their own class but not at home in any other class, they had only their home for refuge, where they had dug in deep and raised high ramparts.

Running into my brother outside those walls, we greeted each other as if we had met in a strange land.

'Noel—'

'Ah—' He was dressed in a suit in the way outdoor types

wear suits, which made him look dressed for pleasure.

'How's business?'

'OK.' He turned to greet a passing Chinese man. 'Tony.'

'Noll. Nice threads.'

'Who's he?' I said.

'A waiter down in the Log Cabin. Lives in the bookies.'

We walked down South William Street together. Noel glanced aside again—'There goes Henry.'

'Wasn't he in class with you?' I looked at the dark-suited man with a briefcase go by, black heavy shoes crunching the grit. 'What's he doing now?'

Noel shrugged, floated away on another digression. Didn't want to be boss, shied from giving orders, taking control; had lost touch with his old school friends—they belonging to the boss class; chatting instead with a Chinese waiter, whomever the water washed by. He stopped outside number 53, bowled a slow imaginary cricket ball, shook his arm loose.

'Are you coming for a drink?'

'Better get back to work.' He glanced at his watch. 'I'll see you tonight.'

'OK. Where?'

'At the staff dance.' He smiled the soft smile of the strong father's son and went up the steps.

But when I looked back he was still standing in the doorway, chatting to an Indian wholesaler with a dozen skirts on his arm.

And maybe he was right, I thought as I went into The Castle. There were Henrys here too, professionals of the arts, advancing their careers step by step. Here comes MacNeil, sultry in a fisherman's gansey.

'Saw your story. Good stuff.'

'Thanks,' I said.

'Part of something longer, is it?'

'I wish.'

'Nothing else coming up?'

'Nope.'

Looking at MacNeill, dreamy-faced, horned with antennae long and feathery as a moth's, I felt the sort of awe mixed with disgust I had when I came across red threads of life in my breakfast egg. This was what life was like, writing too, me, everything; no escape from it, no ducking back through that door into the family business.

'Hi.'

Though she doesn't stand out in my memory, without her my memory is a blur. Like those contraceptive pills she was forever snapping from a numbered tab, Esther is my calendar of that time.

'Morning, Esther.'

She was sitting in the corner, reading a paper, raising it like a shield as I sat down beside her, flicking open her shirt and baring one breast for an instant, covering it again. She smiled— 'What'll you have?'

'Let me.' Incredible that she had been naked in my arms. I tried to picture her so. Couldn't. I went to the counter.

'Morning, Percy.'

Puff.

'Another sherry?'

'No thanks.' Pause. 'It's my birthday.'

'Congratulations.'

'Let the day perish wherein I was born and the night in which it was said—There is a man child conceived ...'

More irritating than amusing lately, that bookish voice. I returned to Esther.

'Who's he? He was trying to come on to me.'

'Percy was?'

She mimicked his voice. 'One may dweam.'

'What did you say?'

'That I was waiting for my boyfriend.'

That line again. Again my cock sat up. Again too, she took out her contraceptive pills, washed one down with Guinness.

'Not much need for those with me.'

'One may dweam ...'

'What are you doing tonight?' I heard myself say suddenly.

'Nothing.' Smiling, winding a black lock of her hair about her finger. 'What do you have in mind?'

I described the family staff dance, heard my voice continue, 'Would you like to come?'

'Why not?' And she went on to talk of books and writing. I went over what I had just said, amazed that I had said it.

'You can't write a novel about Ireland,' Esther was saying. 'Nothing ever happens here.'

Nothing happens? Jamie jumping from a speeding taxi? Bombs in Dublin? Donald beaten up by a docker in a frock? Percy standing up now, patting his flat hat down on his toupee, heading off to his mistress in Sandymount?

But all that, according to Esther, was just the sand and water. To write a novel you needed cement, and there were only two sorts of cement in Ireland: family and church; other experience unmanageable.

'Why do you live here so?'

'It feels ... real.'

We emptied our glasses.

'See you this evening.' She went down South William Street, her heavy hair, her blue-jeaned bottom swaying.

There they were in the Clarence ballroom— my father and Mr Bennett, the new money and the old. Behind Mr Bennett, the remains of his staff, the deserving Protestant poor. Behind my father, his praetorian guard: men and women, some from the west of Ireland, who had been with him from the days of the long march, served their time with him, and now were employed by him, putting up with his moods, loyal to their

[107]

chief as he advanced into alien land—settled in a Fine Gael suburb, sent his sons to the Jesuits, daughter to the Sacred Heart.

'I suppose it's not surprising,' the Reverend Mother observed when my sister ran down a school corridor, 'considering your background.'

The snub brought home, my mother translated it for my father: 'You have enough; you're tempting God.'

Her family produced national-school teachers, priests at a pinch—a class her husband's career had mocked, he doing in one jump over the traces what her family felt should have been done over three steady generations.

'They're so bloody cautious,' he muttered, and pressed on. And now he was sitting down at the head of the table to celebrate another year's achievement.

'Adrian?' Kevin called on me to give my order, taking control in the too-calm way our father did.

Each of my brothers had some trait of our father's, flourishing it like a title deed, implying that the mantle had fallen on him. And my mother? What trait of hers did we claim? From her came my sister's psoriasis. My beady eyes came from hers—flicking over Esther now, taking her in as casually as her fingertip dabbed crumbs from the tablecloth. My mother's piercing glance was instinctive, I knew: it was the country look that saw through thorn hedges, around boreen bends. But Esther blushed, self-conscious in a skirt.

Noel butted in with his order, then lit another Afton Major and sat back in his chair. What was his trait exactly? In a way he had fled or rejected every trait, and in a way he had succeeded. Yet he presided over this with the authority of his father.

'And, sir?'

'I'll have the sole,' I said, and thought to myself that was what I had of my father—the soul; not any old trait but the green shoot.

'Well done,' I added but the waitress had glanced away as my sister's new boyfriend arrived, even later than me.

'Rich.'

He blushed at the name. He had shortened it—as my sister had shortened hers; though if Philomena suggested Catholic Irish, Richard hardly suggested Anglo-Irish, the background he had fled.

Hiding behind a black beard and a beginner's Irish accent, he sat down quickly opposite Celia, talking at once as self-conscious people do, so as to vanish into the general conversation.

'Did you hear Wilson's speech? That's telling them, Mr Kenny.'

'Ah that's only a blind. He gave in to them, he gave in to them.'

'What's this?' my mother said.

'The Ulster workers' strike.'

'Well I don't like that Harold Wilson—the puss on him.'

'You're right, Mrs Kenny.' Rich began to speak quickly, English public-school voice breaking out. 'The unionists understand only one language—'

'Wine anyone?' Kevin tried to change the subject. Too late.

'What language is that?' Celia said.

Scots unionist, Anglo-Irish nationalist looked at each other coolly. The Kennys watched in awkward Irish silence.

'Their own laguage. Force.'

Without comment Celia passed the bottle.

'I'd have said'—Kevin took it, as if taking the baton in a relay race—'that's the IRA's language.'

'Well we all know who taught them.'

'I don't believe it. You don't support the IRA?'

'I see why they exist.'

'Why's that?' Kevin was shoving back his chair.

Rich spoke with the ease of someone indifferent to whether he pleased or not. 'England has no business in Ireland.'

'I'm sorry, I'm not listening to this!' This was a new Kevin, fingering nervously the spotted silk tie Celia had bought for him, standing white-faced away from the table. 'They kill and they destroy!'

'Ssh!' my mother hissed. 'Sit down, love.'

We might have been chatting about shoes so far as the rest of the ballroom was concerned. Managers, staff—they went on talking amongst themselves. We were different, we had skipped a rung in the ladder—hence the confusion. Kevin and Phil had tried their luck with solid doctors' and lawyers' daughters and sons; retired bored or rebuffed. Hence Celia and Rich ... That was it! I wanted to run to the toilet, to jot down this insight, but couldn't miss this row.

'It was the same in Aden, Cyprus, Kenya. Like I say,' Rich got a grip on his accent, 'that's the only language they understand!'

'What? Blowing up innocent people?'

'Dear Jesus.' My mother put a hand over her eyes, glanced about the room through splayed fingers.

'Well, it's being going on as long as I'm alive,' my father turned, the waitress approached again, 'and it'll be going on when I'm gone.'

'Leave it, Rich,' my sister said.

Celia nodded, Kevin sat down. Noel raised his head again, lit another cigarette.

Rich too, I noticed as he set to work with knife and fork, had psoriasis, white scales of it on his hands. It sent me back to reckoning up our family's nervous complaints. Kevin had asthma; Noel's dread of any conflict, trouble, rise in temperature was itself a sort of complaint. And myself? I turned quickly to the kiss-and-make-up conversation my mother had begun.

'Do you see Harry Morton, Dada?'

'I see him. And the straight black trousers down to his shoes.'

'A good rep.' Kevin gave a dry smile.

'I suppose. Considering he has only the one leg.' My father smiled the original of the smile Kevin had attempted. My mother began to laugh as my father lowered his eyes to the tablecloth and began to speak in his super-bland weather forecaster's voice, which meant a funny story.

How warm and easy it was here. Clan easy. A country

priest, a TD, an old Mayo neighbour's son employed now by my father. Even one of the waiters, a drinking friend of long ago to judge by his grey nose, was joining in the party—

'Well, Eddie.'

'Ah, Jim ...'

The band began playing, the old began moving from table to table. Old men from Frawley's stood behind my father, laying hands on his shoulders, confirming the apostolic succession—the poor who had got on but not forgotten their own.

'Didn't I train him well! And how's business, Eddie?'

'We'd be alright if we could get rid of that Coalition.'

'What do you make of that Cruise O'Brien at all?'

'Well we were bad enough without him.'

'Did you see the interview with Haughey last night?'

'They had it in for him.' My father jutting out his jaw, the tough old peasant 'They had it in for him.'

'They have it in for Fianna Fáil.'

'But have they?' I joined in, my voice as floppy as my hair.

'What?' My father turned to me, flushed awkwardly. 'Sure they always had. Didn't they say Seán Lemass lost all his money at cards and had to go to Joe McGrath, and his wife had to sell the silver. And what they didn't say about Dev ...' His toe swung, stirring the white tablecloth.

All hands on deck then to pump out the embarassment—

'Well, Aidreen,' Mr Sinnot said 'And what are you doing at all?'

'Writing.'

'Sure I suppose the boss can afford it—hah? A bit of luxury.'

I turned to Kevin. 'Where's Brian?'

'He's not coming.'

'He's only across the river.'

'On principle.' Kevin smiled, as if he had been trying out one of his Italian business phrases.

'Good,' Celia said—at once praising Kevin for effort, Brian for his principle. 'He's right.'

'Why?' Kevin slipped back into our father's weary patriarch voice-mould.

'He's doing what he believes in.' Celia looked pleased, as if she too had spoken a new tongue.

'True.' Kevin smiled up the table to our mother, turned quickly away from those warm hungry brown eyes, back to Celia. Inch by inch she was stepping away from our mother, from small-talk outings to the Shelbourne where, over tea in an alcove, my mother could ambush with her eyes the passers-by, discuss them with Celia; discuss them and nothing else. Inch by matching inch Kevin was distancing himself, separating Family from Business; as difficult and necessary as separating fact from fiction was for me; as tricky as drawing a twig from a nest without bringing the whole thing down. Oh what a fall that would be, down back into the bog our father had taken us from.

'Where are you from, Esther?'

'New England,' I said. 'Who's Noel with?'

Kevin looked down the floor to where our brother was dancing cheek to cheek. 'Una. She's in Camden Street.'

Celia smiled. 'He's in with a chance there.'

'How can you tell?'

'It's all in the eyes.'

'I can't see it.'

'Ask him in the morning.' Celia paused as she saw Kevin stare. 'Do you not talk about things like that? My brother and I used to have great morning-after sessions.'

'Not us.'

'You Kennys. You're so—'

'Yes—' Again Kevin did our father's voice, smiled up the table. 'A pious mother.'

'Pious my arse—' Celia stopped, as if she had made a mistake, gone too far too soon in this foreign language. Kevin looked away, a frown cleft in his brow, clan loyalty struggling against longing to be free of clan. My younger brother but older in experience, able now to handle a marriage row. Celia frowned and looked in the other direction as if trying to identify what it was about all this that she disliked—something Irish-country-Catholic collective that jarred on her British-city-Protestant self?

But there was Dublin Protestant Mrs Bennett laying down her cigarette-holder, saying, 'Shall we dance, darling?'

'Wish me luck, old man.' Mr Bennett finger-flicked his natty moustache, his black tie, palmed the silver temples sleek and followed his wife onto the floor.

'Isn't he very nice?' my mother said.

'Ah yes,' my father shrug-smiled, off-guard for an instant, a gold fleck of arrogance showing in the smile, 'he's a lightweight.'

Brow clearing, question answered, Celia turned back to the table.

'Isn't it well for her,' my mother's eyes following Mrs Bennett's lopsided whirl, 'she doesn't care who sees her.'

My mother did. Even to stand up, show her head an inch above the crowd, was beyond her. Sitting, she received visitors —Mrs Morgan, Mr Sinnot, foot-soldiers from the hard old days—who came to sit next to her; she putting her hand on their hand as they talked; they not putting their hand on hers. She was the boss's wife, but she was of their world, had worked as a shop assistant—where? That, like the whereabouts of the Cross, was a mystery.

'Take Adrian,' Celia resumed. 'He wants to do something, and he does it. I don't like his writing, I don't agree with Brian's socialism—but I admire them for doing what they believe in.'

'What sort of writing do you like?' Esther spoke at last.

'Something that makes me think. Hermann Hesse. Something that makes me grip my knickers.'

Esther was silent again, looking about, taking it all in. Celia followed her gaze, as if trying to see what those dark-ringed eyes found interesting.

'Do you know who I saw the other day, Mrs Kenny—remember old Deeney?'

'Don't tell me he's alive still, Mrs Morgan?'

'No—remember his son?'

'With the bad back? Ah God he was lovely.'

'He's working down in Boyers.'

'What? And what happened the shop?'

'Gone. Gone wallop. The boss was saying he saw him in Stubbs.'

'Dear Jesus, and he did a great trade.'

Celia gave up with a yawn.

The band was playing reggae now, Noel doing a window-cleaning routine with one hand, other hand on a swaying hip, wide-mouthing the words—

'*Get up in the morning slaving for bread, sir,*
So that every mouth can be fed,
Oh, oh, the Israelite ...'

'Well she's certainly enjoying herself. My God.' My mother rested her hand on Mrs Morgan's hand.

'Why wouldn't she? Dancing with the boss's son!' Mrs Morgan laughed, leaned closer as my mother whispered something. Mrs Morgan replied aloud, 'Una.'

'Look at her whispering away.' Celia paused, as my father had before his dry-smiled comment on Mr Bennett. Then—'She is the most manipulative spider I have ever met.' She returned my mother's wave.

Mrs Morgan was rising now, my mother's hand still holding her hand, getting one last piece of information about a hairdresser or dressmaker—at the same time pressing a ten-pound note folded to postage-stamp size into Mrs Morgan's hand, forcing Mrs Morgan's fingers shut on it. A gift? For Mrs Morgan? For Mrs Morgan's brother, the Capuchin with the drink problem in Church Street? For Mrs Morgan's niece from Galway, another twig in the great nest?

'She's shy,' I said, angry defensive, yet elated too by Celia's cold clarity.

'She's not a bit shy. She just makes you play by her rules. She won't take a step out of that web. She just sits in there waiting for flies to land.'

'Look, we don't talk about your mother like that!'

'Say away! You won't be saying anything I haven't said. When my mother rings me up moaning, I tell her I haven't the slightest sympathy. If she wants to change her life, let her change her life.' Celia's peaky pointed face lit up intensely. 'The happiest day of my life was the day that I left home. I was eighteen ...'

Easy to leave a cold Scots home. But how to leave a den—animal loyalty, animal warmth?

Celia looked at me. 'Of course you like your mother.'

Like? 'Yes,' I said. 'Is that unusual?'

'I wouldn't trust her if she was the last person on earth.'

And the band went on playing, Noel went on dancing with the staff, my sister with her boyfriend Rich; Mr Bennett and his wife did an old-time tango glide; and a hundred others all bopping to the reggae beat—subjects of my father's kingdom. Belshazzar at the feast, he turned as my voice rose—

'Why do you say that?'

'Because she has no life of her own. She sucks it out of others.'

'She has more life than you'll ever have.' I heard my voice fall into my father's calm tone, a sure sign I was rattled.

Calmly my father looked away again.

'She's dead,' Celia pronounced. I felt a flutter of life.

My mother's audiences were over. She turned, looked smiling down our table again—and as if the table had been tilted Kevin turned abruptly to Celia—'Will we dance?'

'If you've got it, flaunt it.'

And they whirled out onto the floor.

My trembling heel tapped to the beat, the beat of what was happening. I looked up the table at my father. What spring long-coiled in that Connaught cottage had driven him here? Or had he ever left it? Was this mixture of clan and commerce, family and employees, country and city, wife and mother just a grotesque inflation of a home he had never left? I studied his face: slack eyelids making blue eyes dark, upper lip thinned by disappointment, determination. I felt my own mouth tighten into a similar line as an awful question tiptoed across my mind.

To be like him, would we have to break him?

'But I don't want to end up like Bonnie and Clyde
Ohohoh the Israelite …'

'Aw shoot!'

Those words again; and then those other words as familiar, breathed on my bare shoulder: 'You're very nice.'

'I'm sorry.'

'Don't be.' Esther settled her head into the crook of my arm.

I sing of failure and love, of those nights together talking, or reading whatever was at the bedside—my Roget's thesaurus, her Emily Dickinson—until she slept. I lay awake longer, falling slowly into sleep through thoughts as ordered as Roget, as tangled as Esther's black hair which her breathing brushed up, down my shoulder.

In some similar gradual sudden way I woke next morning—as Esther stirred and light lines sharpened between the venetian blind slats—my mind made up to leave home, clear out, up sticks, shove off, make tracks, sling my hook, cut and run.

— 9 —

Pitying our past self is as pointless as pitying our present. We can't, won't, have it any different. We move like the sea, infinitely aimless and effective, breaking up what can be broken, washing over what can not.

Nothing—not my digs, Lancashire 1973, not the red Walls sausage on blue earthenware hand-thrown by the landlady, not the hot brown bedroom where I sat down before my typewriter in the evening—nothing could break up that novel.

One morning I found an earwig on the typewriter. When I tried to brush him off he ran into the works. I couldn't shake him out and I sat with a sentence in my head, afraid that the first letter might strike him dead. In the same way I was afraid of finishing my novel. It threatened the living earwig inside me.

'The path—winding deep between banks of tangled grass, studded yellow with primroses, threaded too with trefoil—led to ...'

Jesus H. Christ—as Esther used to say—what was I doing? I was driving with the brakes on, sailing with the anchor down, every word dragging a clause. But still, I was another few chapters nearer the end—and another year older.

My mother drifted into the study. 'Take care would you tell them what you're doing.'

I rested an elbow on the typewriter. 'What am I doing?'

'Can't you say you're a teacher?'

'I'm not. I left. I left.'

'Jesus—can't you say it?'

The doorbell rang.

I was home again, back in that land of baffling kindness and quick wits, the colours beige and fawn.

Other emigrants were home too: my father's family, old, rich enough now to visit the country they had not seen or wanted to see for thirty, forty years. My father—youngest son, the richest one—was host and enjoying it. They were family, the only air he could breathe for long, and yet by now they were outsiders too—an ideal mixture.

His sister Rita, rooted in New York since the First War, living with her friend, husky-voiced Bess, since the Second: they were staying in the Shelbourne, coming to our house each evening for dinner. Through open doors I could hear them denounce a film they had seen—*Ryan's Daughter.*

His brother Joe—took off to New Jersey in the twenties, vanished for thirty years into an underworld of drink, surfaced in middle age married to an Italian widow: in matching lightweight suits, supporting each other's elbows, they walked up and down one side of the back garden, stopping by each standard rose tree and saying to each other—'Boy, isn't that something.'

While on the other side, his sister Nellie—sailed to Spain in 1926, entered a convent there and vanished until the Second Vatican Council 'sprung her', as Bess would say after her second cocktail—Sister Nellie walked up and down reading Vespers, not quickening her step as my mother knocked on the window, called 'Yo-hoo!' to announce the yellow melon cocktail.

The doorbell rang again, family members clocked in, standing-room only in the sitting-room. The views of Stephen's Green from the Shelbourne, of Galway Bay from the Eglinton, were compared. Bess threw back a vitamin B with her highball. Joe tried a shot of Seven-Up.

'You might bring Joe and Maria for a drive after dinner,' my mother murmured to me. 'Out to the sea or somewhere.'

'Do they want to go?'

'I'll go.' Noel said he wasn't doing anything. Nor was he, nor could he. Kevin was married, had taken on our father's family-business mantle. Noel was single, stuck in the role of son. 'I'll go,' he repeated.

Not what my mother wanted. Why not? How was Noel alone with Joe and Maria dangerous to family security?

Why not send Kevin? Because he was married to a Protestant?

But Celia had become a Catholic, was studying her new religion with cool detachment.

'Noel could take them in Dada's car,' Kevin said, 'and I can drive you into town in mine.'

'I will.' Celia had her own car now.

'OK.' Noel smiled his father's dry smile.

Metternich at Vienna, my mother hesitated. She turned to me—'Would you ever ring the gong?'

Suddenly I was in the hall before the gong, another of our father's auction-room finds—brass face supported by a brazen serpent, its forked tongue the gong-stick's rest; beaten only on family tribal occasions; beaten by me now in rage at what was happening, in joy at what was happening, at the loosening of another coil in the family business; beating it so hard that the mahogany stick snapped.

'You ought to see a doctor'—my mother appeared behind me, pressed a hand on the gong, quenching its vibration—'for your nerves.'

'I am. Celia recommended—'

'Don't you ever tell Celia *anything*.'

'Why not?'

'That's the why, dear.' Calm collapsing then before my stare, my middle-class educated stare. Calmness, doing, saying what you wanted—all that was for the strong, the rich, the edu-cated. She came from the weak, the poor. Their strength was in staying together, their greatest threat was exile from the flock, the clan. 'Or I'll never speak to you as long as you live.' Her face paled, she vanished into the kitchen.

After fifty years in Spain Sister Nellie could hardly speak English, but all the Irish emigrant traits were there still in that tiny black-habited figure stammering 'Sí! Sí! Sure I remember eet well—at ze end of the ze bog road ...'

There was the memory of Home, the pleasure in living far from it. She was leaving next week, for ever. So were Joe, Rita ... never to return. They were in good spirits.

'That's what I call a garden.' Joe looked out the window at the apple trees. I looked at the back of Jamie's house beyond. Joe stroked the table's amber surface and spoke of life during the Depression. In Philadelphia, working as a milkman—the frost so hard, the hill so steep—he had to lay his coat over the ice for the horse to grip on.

'Fff!' My mother got up. 'That was some job I can tell you.'

'Then I got a job in a diner ...'

'There's more mayonnaise ...' My mother escaped to the kitchen. Much as she liked company, for her it was a stone thrown in the pool, upsetting her dream of Home.

'Mayo,' Joe said. 'That's what we call it in the States.'

'And how did you find Mayo?' My mother returned. 'Now, eat up every scrap of that!'

'Boy, there sure are some changes there. Boy, there sure are.'

'I couldeent unzerstan whet zey were e-seying,' Nellie said.

'Will you have some more salmon?'

'Sí.'

Rita resumed talking about *Ryan's Daughter*. The most offensive scene of all was the English army officer making love to an Irish girl.

Celia smiled.

Rita didn't. Didn't like Celia. She turned to Family. 'Did you see it, Kevin?'

'We saw it in London.'

Perhaps that was it, I thought as I saw his face turn to Celia even while he spoke to Rita—as Perseus looked at the Gorgons by means of a mirror: together, they were too strong for him, these peasant relatives, this circle of identical hook noses and cloudy blue eyes, although, like the Gorgons, they seemed to share one eye, the Family eye.

Rita who had nursed Legs Diamond king of the underworld when he was shot, and become his friend. Joe who had survived another underworld. Nellie who had dressed as a boy and fled over the Pyrenees when Republican troops advanced on her convent. What lives they had had. Yet how little life of their own they had. Rita—a spinster nurse. Nellie—a nun. Joe—a drunken bachelor until middle age when he married an Italian Mama. I thought of their other brothers and sisters: Petie, a bachelor, Margaret, a spinster, Mae—poor Mae who wanted to be buried in the same coffin as her mother and was killing the time till then drinking red wine. They had left home in body but never in spirit. In fact, only my father had married someone his own age, cast adrift from the family web, spun a single gossamer line of his own. How precious it was. I felt it tremble as Celia cut in—

'How's England?' She addressed me in the voice one adult uses to another above babbling children.

'Eat up, Celia,' my mother said. Too late. Rita had heard.

'You were in England?'

'In Lancashire.'

'That's where father used to go ...'

My mother seized the digression. 'Oh hadn't they the hard life, setting off—'

Rita pressed on. 'Were you long there, Adrian?'

'No. I left.'

'How's Roderick at all?' My mother turned again. 'He met this boy he knew at uni—'

'He's'—living alone over a shop, building a model of an eighteenth-century ship on the kitchen table—'grand', I said.

'And where did you go then?'

'Germany.'

'What were you doing there?'

'Nothing.'

My mother held on to the table. 'He was staying with Anthony Gorman, this boy he knew at school. Anthony's a historian, isn't that right?'

'Yes—' he's studying German and sleeping with women.

'Joe,' Rita called across the table, 'wasn't our Nan in Germany?'

'Who?'

'Our sister Nannie. Wasn't she in Germany after the War?'

'Wheech warr?'

My mother pressed a finger into this hole opening in the family dam. 'Kevin, weren't you there once, that time you were buying the Romika shoes?'

Kevin nodded. 'And where did you go then?'

'Turkey, Iran ...'

Rita interrupted again—'Why would you want to go to Iran. I remember Bob—'

'Who ees Bob?'

'Nan's son. Bob was there with Shell and she said he thought he'd never get home ...'

England, Germany, Iran ... They had been there before me, my family, my home.

'Now eat up—there's plenty more.' My mother went back to the kitchen where she broke quietly into song, an old air from home, from long ago—

'*One morning in June, agus me dul a spaisteoireacht ...*'

At the head of the table my father was looking at his watch. Fifty minutes until the next TV news. Nothing more to do. Energy throbbing in his temple vein. He turned to me—'Will you grind the coffee?' He wanted to draw me into this Medusa tangle of sisters and brothers he hardly knew. 'Sure he's a little old man,' he had smiled to me when Joe appeared from the taxi. Getting back no smile from me.

'They're your family,' my no-smile said, 'not mine.'

Burnt into him—as he watched his mother weep and wave her children one by one, year by year, into the train and out of sight forever—an image of poverty, scattering, heart-breaking home-breaking. This home, this family business was his reply to that past, I knew even as I stood up, suddenly smothering—

'I won't bother with coffee, thanks. I'm going out to see—' Who? Who? 'Percy.'

'Who?' My mother snapped wide-awake, vaulted over the corral of Spanish and American chat.

'Pursey?' Maria said.

'Yeah—Perzy!' Joe called into her good ear.

They were all awake at once, interested. They bored each other stiff, I thought as I slipped away. From the corner of my eye I saw Celia give me an adult smile.

Percy was alone, sitting on his Arts and Crafts stool—a square of old Irish yew with a spar for a back—in the small sitting-room, made smaller by Big House remains: family portraits, painted display-cabinet that grazed the ceiling, glass-domed Empire clock—its pendulum a golden swing on which a golden cherub rocked back and forth, its tick-tock and the purr of the cat curled on Percy's lap the only sounds.

'Each friend's death links us to eternity.' Puff. 'I'm practically living there now.'

His wife had died. He had called her Mama.

'Now what are you going on about?' A woman came in and set a tray of bottles on a table, cleared away the latest folder-full of Percy's journal.

'You've met Jane?'

'He hasn't.' She cut off Percy's introductions. 'I'm his bloody housekeeper.' She went out to the kitchen again.

Pause. 'What do you think?'

'She's different,' I said.

'Isn't she.' Smile, blank as the cat's.

'You're not—?' A rush of interest envy rage.

Sip. 'Sacrifice—as Casanova would say—has been offered on the altar of Venus.'

'Percy, how old are you?'

'Seventy-seven.' Smile. 'Too old for her. I'm afraid she may … flit the coop.' Puff. 'I don't suppose you'd be interested in … entertaining her?'

'Howdoyoumean?'

'There's a guest bedroom.'

The doorbell rang. Jane went to answer it.

'Do.' Percy said. 'I wouldn't like to lose her.'

His weekly At Home began—a mixture of Beetle Drive, pub, and gossip-column people. It gave me the same hysterical, boxed-in feeling my own family gave me. A blast of fresh air as a drunken novelist kicked Percy's painted cabinet, shouted, 'How can you bear to live with this junk!'

Percy watched with the same Egyptian mummy smile that he wore when offering his housekeeper to me—or me to his housekeeper? That he wore listening to a purple-cheeked civil servant cry into his ear—'So I showed the story to Frank O'Connor, and he said—I always remember what he said, and this was in 1942, the second of February 1942—You haven't been wasting your time, he said …'

Roger the American was chattering like a jay about the Tichborne scandal. Again. A famous writer of cookery recipes was explaining how alive she felt in New York. Her husband nodded, said it was to do with the electricity in the air.

'Did you feel alive there?' She turned to him.

'Yes, darling, I really felt transformed.'

In the buzz I watched a Catholic intellectual with leather elbow patches draw a thorn from the back of his hand with a safety pin. I was waiting for a pause, to take my leave smoothly, when the door opened again and Jane showed in—

'Hi—'

'*Esther*—'

She was dressed as ever, in jeans and that shapeless jersey which somehow suggested the full figure beneath.

'You're back.' She sat down beside me and we slipped into easy warm chat, as if we really were … At Home.

'What are you doing here?'

'What are you?'

'I have to get out now and then.'

'I'm not surprised.'

'It's not that bad.' She smiled her sleepy smile. She was still living in half a room in Upper Leeson Street. 'I've done it up. I'll show you … later.'

As always my cock sat up. Her ease was catching. Now, suddenly, I was transformed, the one prolonging pleasurable anticipation.

Tonight I felt confident somehow. Tonight … at last. It was a pleasure now to listen to a TV raconteur with a cravat and a well-tooled Dublin accent tell again what Behan had said to him. Percy listened, face impassive—Saint Sebastian as another arrow went home.

Arm in arm we walked to the bus stop, got the upstairs front seat, still chatting easily as the bus coasted in the Rock Road.

Across the bay the dark blue shape of Howth Head melted into dark blue sky.

'Why does the last bus always go so fast?'

'I suppose it's like a horse when you turn back for home.'

'Will we go back to your place?'

She linked my arm. 'Have you a better idea?'

As we turned up the canal bank I realized that I had. Stephen was in London covering the latest Anglo-Irish talks— and no doubt seeing Helen too. I still had a key to his flat. There was a double bed, maybe a drop of wine.

The same brown silent hall, the numbers scribbled about the pay phone, the narrow top flight of stairs.

Flowers withering in a green-scummed milk bottle, a grain

of dope in a twist of silver paper, the *TLS* fallen open on the floor somehow in an igloo shape. Esther sat down, rolled a joint, looked around. 'What does he do?'

'He's a journalist.' I sat beside her
Long kisses, delicious, with pauses for conversation.

'Have you been doing anything?'

'Trying.' She drew off her pullover, I mine.

'Can I hear something?'

Stephen's bedroom was the same, still carpeted in fluff, the mirror veiled with dust, the postcard of Fra Angelico's Annunciation still cockling on the mantelpiece. Esther sat on the side of the bed, reciting in her slow New England voice as she undressed—

> '*We give things names to tame them*
> *To separate our skins from pain*
> *Thinking the taste of words*
> *Will ease our fear;*
> *We speak believing sounds*
> *Will shelter us from death and rain*
> *Afraid of loneliness ...*'

I looked at her, her deep yellow breasts studded with those tiny nipples, black hair tangled by drawing off her clothes. Tonight she was the one delaying. It only increased my desire. She smiled at it, sat still as if following some strand of her own thought. 'Maybe we give things names to make them real?'

'Maybe.'

'And if there's no name for it, does that mean it's nothing?'

'Mmm?' Standing, still erect, feeling ridiculous, I saw Helen's old blue silk dress on the bedside chair, thrown away by her, or set there by Stephen in her memory. Stoned? Cold? I hung it on my shoulders. It breathed out still Helen's expensive perfume. Vaguely smiling, Esther stood up naked. 'Why did you do that?' Her hand stroked the silk.

I shrugged off the dress, drew her to me.

'No—really, why?' She rested her cheek on my shoulder and looked out the window: a view of night sky, a distillation of greys; moon slipping through grey cloud, cloud wisps closing again, oozing up into great shapes ... river ... horseman ... a shock-headed angel; followed by a spat of rain, stopping again, the cloud lightening a tone, darkening again; a hundred shades of grey locked in one straining mass.

'I don't know.' Again I drew her to me.

'You ought to know something.' She drew back, eyes shining with tears as well as laughter, her voice with the distinctive tone of something never spoken before. 'I prefer girls.'

The clouds parted again and full moonlight surged in the window, spangling her black bush with silver.

WICKLOW HARBOUR

− 10 −

Wind out of a black sky was rushing snow up Dawson Street, throwing open the door as I turned the handle, moaning across the floor.

'I'd like to buy a house.'

'Plenty of those.' Wine-inflamed face, estate agent's voice. He looked out at the blizzard as I went through a red plastic folder.

Overlooking Wicklow Harbour—£4,000.

The sum my father had lodged in my bank account three years before. 'I'll take that one,' I said.

'That's a nice one.' Smile withdrawing as I took out my chequebook.

'Who'll I make this out to?'

'Have a look at it first.' He laid an understanding hand on mine.

28 JANUARY 1975. Moved to Wicklow ... It was a terraced house—two down, two up. From the front bedroom you could see across the harbour and the bay beyond, a line brought to a green full stop by Bray Head. Again I opened up the card-table and set the typewriter on top.

A warning rattle of TV gunfire from next door, but I was too busy unpacking to notice. As soon as the bed was up I fell asleep, dreaming of rising early next morning to write, write the book. The Book.

A noise at midnight like barrels falling from a cliff-top, electric light filled the room. A ship had entered the harbour, her hold covers were falling open. Through the next seven hours I listened to the crane-generator throb as she unloaded. I dozed at dawn, was woken by a radio next door. I sat out on the side of the bed and wept.

Outside, the ship was sailing away, dirty courtesy flag flapping in a breeze. Back to Casablanca for another load of phosphates, said one of the men leaning on the sea wall. Only a coaster, they said. Old sailors, they passed the day there watching the traffic of the sea. They talked of ships that took a week to unload. I went back inside my red-brick cell, to black coffee and a blank page.

To unload my own cargo, whatever that was, I needed silence, dark throbbing infinite silence. Through the wall, from next door, came the Gay Byrne programme. My neighbour was an old woman alone. After morning radio she turned on TV for the rest of the day—and night, I knew with sudden certainty. The telephone rang—my father asking how I was settling in. His concern filled the room. I went out for a walk, the first of my endless walks, that always led back to the harbour. I was trapped.

Those endless walks inland. Mind strung tight. Walking walking, Kenny's shoes eating up the tarmac of East Wicklow. Grey stone walls, blackthorn and hazel hedges self-seeding out into fields. Brownwater streams growling alongside, vanishing under the road. Wet clouds half the size of the sky sliding into one another not far above. Stopping on a moss- and fern-dressed bridge, staring down into the bubble and foam-skinned torrent, watching a white polythene fertilizer bag tug-tugged from the barb of wire that was snagging it; tugged tugged and would be tugged until the polythene rotted in ten, twenty years' time.

Walking faster. A farmer leaning against a tractor, straightening a wire coat-hanger for some purpose that bothered him, looked up at me speed by and called in the shocking-healthy voice of the outdoor—'Isn't it well for you! And not a care in your head!'—and bent his own head back to the wire. The roadside wall winding uphill to rusted green gates, creaking open into a hilltop graveyard.

In loving memory of Annabel Palmer daughter of William Palmer of Fairyhill departed this life ...

Lichen blotting the date, a sidewall of the tomb cracked open, bones scattered on moss of ringing green. Picking one up—a broken femur—striding out again, talking to myself—'Help me Annabel Palmer to live'—clutching the dead bone in my pocket.

Off my rocker, on the road, walking till evening sometimes, stopping at some guesthouse—Rathdrum, Aughrim. Joining in the chat after dinner with the residents—a substitute teacher, an agricultural adviser. Wonderful chat, mixed with my leapfrog thoughts.

'Awful night that in the North last night.'

'Cat.'

'Lined them up against the fucking van and shot them.'

'Fucking cat.'

—Cioran says we exist only by refusing free rein to our supreme desire.

'Well, Joe, do any good last night?'

'Do any bad, you mean.'

'Where was he?'

'Arklow.'

—Man, equally alien from the being of nature and the doing of the machine, the vile becoming.

'Oh lashings of hole in Arklow.'

—Stop thinking. Look, look at him sniffing his fingers, listen to what he's saying. Listen!

'What sort of soap is that in the toilet at all?'

'That's Arklow soap!'

'Shouldn't be putting your hand in places like that, Joe.'

—Laugh. Go on laugh.

'Hahaha!'

'And where are you from yourself?'

'... Wicklow.'

'You got a right soaking.'

'I was walking.' I clutched Annabel Palmer's legbone.

'And could you not get a lift?'

—Relax. Why are you sweating? He's going.

'Which way are you going?'

'Back to Wicklow.'

'Do you want a lift? It's lashing.'

'Lift back to Wicklow. Dark. Silence except for the splash of rainfall and ducks paddle-quacking in a back yard ...'

Sweating getting into bed, turning the light out, on again, writing in my notebook again.

'Why do you write instead of living? Stop writing. Let go. Let go the dead bone ...'

Withdrawing to the room farthest from the harbour and the old woman next door, to the back bedroom. But there, clearer than ever now, I could hear the harbour noise, the Gay Byrne housewife laughter. Putting up a partition wall; the noise still creeping in. Laying down three inches of newspaper under the carpet. But still the noise from abroad, the voices from home.

How? Through the window. *Yes.*

'Isn't he very fond of himself.' The old woman next door smiled as my double-glazing went in. She was fond of me. Each time I asked her to turn down the TV or radio, I gave her a present—a cake or jam. She preferred the cakes, she said.

But now the trickle of noise coming in was deafening. Deafening as my wrist watch. Soon I was locking it in the hot-press before I sat down to write. What a book this would be. *What a book.* Each word cemented into place like a stone. One evening the silence was ripped open by a thunder under the carpet, where I found a mouse nibbling the newspaper—so shocked by my scream that he stood rigid. I took him by the neck and set him outside the double-glazing, on the window sill. He must have jumped. Next morning he was gone.

Inspecting the harbour each morning. Going to bed if a ship was in. Sleeping with earplugs, sometimes all day—through Gay Byrne, the Angelus, Little House on the Prairie, Racing from Newmarket, Today Tonight, Nightlight and the National Anthem. Getting up as the bats came out and the old woman next door went to bed. Looking out at the harbour. Ship gone. No new ship in. So I had my breakfast, and by one o'clock in the morning was sitting down to my day's work in silence.

Such silence. Pure black as sea and sky. I was writing flash-backs now. The hero was walking about the city still, but I had run out of ideas for him. To keep him walking, I was giving him memories of childhood. He was walking backwards, but still walking.

There was the terror-thought, plaiting my long motionless sentences, that I wasn't unloading but lashing down the cargo; but I went on rowing my stone boat, while the tide made, then ebbed from the sea wall below—until daybreak when I went for my evening walk and watched the seals play in the morning sun, returned at breakfast time and had my supper, and then to bed.

★

Somehow then the next step.

One day when a ship came in—the Leviathan the old seamen had foretold, a Liberian giant that would take a week to unload—I rose from the typewriter, from that deep dark silence before the double-glazing began to vibrate from the crane-generator throb, walked out the door to the railway station and took the train up to Dublin.

'Percy.'

Percy stood up fold by fold, more like a carpenter's rule now.

An old man with a boy's face stayed sitting, cleaning a fingernail with a thumbnail.

'I've told you about Nicholas. Nicholas Wyse.'

The old man put out a hand through Percy's introductions—

'Hello.'

'Hello, Mr Wyse.'

'Don't call him that,' Percy mumured, 'he won't know who you're talking about.' Then—that selfishness I envied—he wavered out the door.

'An assignation.'

'How does he do it?'

'Have you ever seen any of them?' Nicholas pressed fingertips to temples in gentle horror. Gentleman's soft hands, dented pale even by that contact with his forehead. Gentleman's voice and confident easy silences. A frayed tip of violet silk handkerchief in his breastpocket the only fleck of colour. Another ancient monument for me to hide behind. But an artist too—

'But'—grimace—'I didn't have the stuff.'

Through the plot of my novel, doing cartwheels in my head, I made conversation. 'What stuff?'

'Talent.'

'Hasn't Percy something of yours?' I remembered a picture that had caught my eye, clumsy simple as the name signed in a schoolboy hand below. I described it: two charcoaled lovers cocooned in a white chalk bed like a cloud.

'That's right. I gave it to him. He'd given me a book of his'—Nicholas tilted his eyes—'*pensées*.'

'You don't like them?'

'*Lovers like burglars walk at night*.' Nicholas mimicked like a schoolboy behind the teacher's back. He fumbled his cuff back from his watch. 'Which way are you going?'

'Nowhere, really.'

'I've a book out. I want to see if it's in the shops.'

Rheumatic old feet in loose-laced shoes, dabbing watering eyes with his violet hankie, he led the way up Nassau Street.

'What is it?'

'Memoirs.' Grimace again. 'Those who can't, write memoirs.'

'Failure is as interesting as success.' I tried the adult voice.

'Then I'm very interesting.' He went into Hanna's. The book was flat on a ledge. Nicholas stood the top copy upright. It fell over.

'What's it about?' I opened it, stood it upright again.

'What do you think?'

'Not Joyce?' Percy had mentioned this friendship with the master.

Nicholas nodded—so vaguely that Mr Hanna, coming down the shop sprinkling water on the floorboards, approached in reply.

'It's moving, Mr Wyse.' His tone respectful of Nicholas as gentleman, not author. He laid the top book flat again, shuffled it square with the others. 'Would you'—turning to me, grey toothbrush moustache a-bristle—'tell your father his apples are falling into my garden.'

'Your plums are falling into ours.'

'I see.' Taking up his tin can, Mr Hanna resumed his war on dust. 'I see.'

'We're next-door neighbours,' I explained.

'Plums are better.' Smiling, walking on tender feet as if on thin ice, Nicholas led the way to the next shop, the next. No sign. 'That's it.' He gave his shrug.

'There's one more. The APCK.'

He walked up Dawson Street slowly. 'What do you make of him—Joyce?'

'Great.'

Past the wine-faced estate agent still looking out his window like Procrustes.

'The *Portrait* can be a pain in the arse,' I added, blood still warm from my little spat with Mr Hanna.

'I think it's his best.'

'But all that putting-down of everyone to elevate Stephen Hero? It makes the Church seem a riot of pagan freedom.'

'That's why it's great.' Nicholas stopped for breath.

'So art is power?'

'No. They're as different as … apples and plums.' Smiling, showing a gold tooth. 'Have you a temper?'

'I'm afraid so.'

'That's a good sign.'

'Here we are.' I pushed open the door.

'Isn't this'—he spoke uneasily as we entered—'a Christian place?'

'There it is anyway.'

There was his book, standing face-out opposite the door.

There in the bow window was the sallow-faced girl I used to see passing my flat in Oakley Road at night. So this was where she worked.

'Hello.'

'Hello.'

'Don't buy it,' Nicholas said. 'I'll give you a copy.'

'Thanks.' I stood still.

Nicholas glanced at me, at her, then nodded and walked out slowly—the door swinging back cold air.

★

'Hello.'

'Hello again.'

'Would you like to have a drink with me after work?'

'Yes.'

Waiting for her in the tiny basement bar up the street, I chatted with Colin.

'Colin, were you ever in love?'

'Once.' Colin paused for so long that I turned to look at him: the same old butterfly-bright bow tie, grey goatee waxed into two yellowish tips.

'What was it like?'

'It was along a river. And there was love. And it was beautiful.' Colin stopped talking and—like a stretched elastic released—sprang back to flippancy, taking a beer mat, skimming it across the counter at the bar boy.

'Hello.' She came in.

'Colin, this is Ruth.'

Colin nodded, flicked another beer mat.

'Will we sit over here?'

'Or would you rather stand?'

'You've been standing all day.'

'Try walking,' Colin said.

'How about the Shelbourne?'

'If you want to.' Her voice irritated me. Submissive.

'You don't like it?'

'I've never been in it.'

'What do you think?'

She looked around. 'It's like Italian ice cream.'

'Will we stay?'

'Don't you like it?'

'I've been to three family reunion dinners here this year.'

[139]

'You don't like your family?'

'Yes. Do you?'

'I don't have one.'

'Here's the waitress.'

'A glass of brandy please.' Not submissive.

'I've seen you before,' I said.

'I know. I've seen you.'

'Walking down Oakley Road?'

'No.'

'Where?' I said.

'Rathmines.'

'Do you live in Rathmines?'

'I used to.'

'So did I.'

'I know.' She drank the brandy in two swallows.

'Will you have another?'

She peeped at her watch. 'No, thank you.'

'You have to meet someone?'

'I have to visit someone.'

'Where did you live in Rathmines?' I walked with her along the Green.

'Rathmines Road.'

'What part?'

'At the top of Cowper Road.'

'That's where I grew up.'

'I know.'

'I don't remember you ...' I looked at her as she turned to a bus that was coming, saw suddenly so clearly through twenty years a skinny girl in a navy gabardine—long sallow jaw, dark hair clipped short—turning to look up Rathmines Road for a 14 bus that was not coming; then recognized her. 'You lived in one of those big houses opposite the bus stop?'

'In a bit of it.' She put out her hand. 'The top flat.'

'I remember you now.'
She nodded once.
'Can I see you again?'
She nodded again.

Down to Wicklow Harbour in the dark then. Then down down down to that dark pit of silence, like a coal mine. An hour sometimes to get down, *really down*; another hour to get through the maze of galleries to where I had left off; hours then chipping, the typewriter rattling like a pick. And not to surface: that was the thing, to stay down even when the work was over, breathe in that dark silence even when eating, walking. Enlarging that perfect airless chamber.

The surfacing now was the going up to Dublin; the train was the cage carrying me up up—Greystones ... Blackrock ... stepping out dazed into the light of Westland Row. To join the two—that was my novel: to join the dark pit and the light.

'Hello.'
    'Would you like to have dinner with me after work?'
    'Yes.'

'Did you visit your someone last week?'
    'Yes.'
    'Can I ask who?'
    'My mother.'
    'You don't live with her now?'
    'No.'
    'Does she still live in that flat?'
    'Yes.'

'You don't say much.'

'I feel nothing but pity for my mother.'

'That's the longest sentence you've spoken to me.'

She drank her glass of brandy in the same two swallows.

Down down down to Wicklow. Down down down into the silent still perfect world. Each tap-tap deepening that black pit. Monday-Tuesday-Wednesday-Thursday-Friday ... Up up up then into daylight Dublin, that was growing brighter. To join the two, that was my novel; to join the two, that was my life. To join the dark pit and the light.

'Are you free after work?'

  'Yes.'

  'Where will we go?'

  'Would you like to have dinner with me?'

  'That's the second longest sentence you've said.'

A dreary narrow road, house, hall, stairs and at the top a dreary narrow room. A smell of damp, a sense of confinement—or, in its bareness, of freedom. The only decoration—Evie Hone's Head of Christ thumb-tacked to the wallpaper, the black and rose ink-wash face a mask of emptiness, or fulfilment.

  'This is where you live?'

  'This is where I exist.' She vanished into a kitchen.

  I snooped about. A blackthorn stick. A shelf of books—Bible, Sophocles, Akhmatova ...

  'I forgot something—' She put her head about the door.

  'Who's Akhmatova?'

  But she had gone down the stairs.

  I drew Akhmatova from the tight-packed shelf, read the lines marked by tiny pencil strokes—

'Who cares for victory? To endure is all ...'
  'I raise my glass ... to the harsh realities: that the world is brutal and coarse, that God in fact has not saved us ...'

'This is all they had.' She held the bottle of wine with both hands.
  'That's dear.'
  She went into the kitchen again, I drew out another book—
Sartre's *Iron in the Soul*. A woman in tweed suit, bunned
silver hair, clear puritan skin—a cartoonist's Protestant lady—
appeared on the stairs, looked at me sitting on the edge of the
bed, then went down again, head-bowed silent.
  'Who's that?' I went into the kitchen. Ruth was on her
knees spooning brown liquid off the lino. She opened the oven
door, more poured out. She put down the spoon, picked up
the cookery book. 'I've done something wrong.'

'You're going to miss your train,' she said.
  'It doesn't matter. I can stay at home.'
  'It's late.'
  'I have a key.' I sat down. 'Or would you like me to go?'
  'Miss Bell would.'
  I stood up. 'Why do you live here? It's awful.'
  'I told you—I exist here.'
  'Sorry—why do you exist here?'
  'I couldn't live at home.'
  'Your mother—does she know where you live?'
  She shook her head, fidgeted about the room, pressing
books back into the shelf.
  'So you're hiding from your mother?'
  'I suppose.'
  I put my arms about her, she began to tremble and I heard a
clink of metal. A frightening image ... a maim repaired ... flick-
ered by my mind's eye. Then as she drew away, a shirt button

[143]

coming undone, I glimpsed a silver cross and chain between beautiful gold-skinned breasts. I took my arms away and she stood in the corner, fidgeting now with the blackthorn stick.

'You're not going to hit me?' I did my blasé smile.

She looked as if she was going to cry. She shook her head.

'Can I see you again?'

'If you can bear to.'

I woke to the hall-door slam, the heavy rev of my father's car. White fringed bedspread, the back of Jamie's house: I was home. Dither dither—and I went down to the breakfast room.

My mother was sitting at the table, looking out at the back garden. The white candle burned, flame still-pale as the bust of the Virgin. Again I caught that scent of peace. The sitting-room clock struck ten as usual. She half turned, her face profiled against the garden's green, almost smiling, as if listening to the chimes; fingernails working away peeling a piece of garlic, slicing it and spreading it on wheatbread. A piece fell to the floor. Addressing it—'Well may you never ...'—she stooped to pick it up, saw me—'Jesus!'—clapped a hand to her breast, as if covering her nakedness.

'Morning.'

'Where did you spring from?' She went out to the kitchen, returned with a knife.

'I came in last night.'

She moved about, setting my place. I moved about too, not able either to be still. What did I fear in her, she in me?

I studied the litter on the table: *Feet of Clay* by Fr Pascal Spellman ... an aerogramme from a never-seen second cousin in California ... a rosehead in a cup of water. The candle burned for the Virgin, but for this too. From here she ruled her kingdom, here was the seat of her power—this oval clawfoot table, this altar to innocence. In the sunlight its polished surface was a pool of amber water.

'No news?' She yawned.

'No.' I yawned back.

'I'm meeting Celia for lunch in town. They were in England.'

'Again?'

'A mini-break, they call it. Where's the Cotswolds at all?'

'The West of England.'

'Sure that's it. The West Country, Kevin said. I didn't know what he meant.' She dabbed dead a greenfly fallen from the rosehead, bit again into the garlic and bread. The candle burned still-pale, sanctioning what she did. Sometimes the flame was shaken—a week of tears and blackmail hysteria when I stopped going to Mass, more tears of reflex piety when a neighbour's daughter got pregnant unwed—and then that healthy peasant gizzard got to work, grinding it all down, assimilating the new, and the flame burned straight and still again.

'Where were you last night?' Offhand.

'I met someone.' Twice as offhand.

Pause. Then—'Remind me to quench that candle. Dada's terrified I'll go out and leave it burning.'

'Would God burn your house down?' I edged the conversation towards the general.

'No. He never let me down.'

'Never?'

'Never. Everything I ever asked Him, He gave me.'

'What did He give you?'

'More than you'll ever know, dear.'

'How can I know if you don't tell me.'

'Didn't He stop your father drinking?'

'How?'

'He gave him the strength.'

'He didn't drink that much.'

'Didn't he?'

'I don't know. Did he?'

'Well, I stayed with him one night before we were married—'

'What?'

Pinking but pushing ahead with her story '—I sat by his bed one night. God only knows what Mrs Thornton thought—'

'Who?'

'His landlady. I can see her yet, looking up the stairs at me. I was mortified. But he was raving. I was afraid to leave him. He wanted to jump out the window—*he thought he could fly.*' She touched tears from her eyes. 'I stayed there till morning, and then I got him into hospital.'

'Why did you never tell me that?'

'I never told anyone that. And don't you—'

'I won't.'

'—ever write that.'

'What happened then?'

'He took the pledge when he came out, and never to this day did he drink a drop … I prayed it out of him,' she added in a murmur tinged with a hiss, then bit into the raw garlic, as if to stop herself from speaking any more.

Unable to stop myself speaking, looking out the window at Mr Hanna's plums rotting into our grass, I said, 'I was with a girl I like last night.'

'I was thinking that.' She blew out the candle with a smile. The dead greenfly vanished over the edge of the table.

'I'm going. I want to get the early train.'

'Can't you come in and say hello to Celia.'

'Where are you meeting?'

'Brown Thomas.'

Hot air, a scent of perfume, soft carpets. My mother was on guard. Anywhere except at home or in a church she was on guard.

'Do you see that one?' she muttered in my ear, tugged my sleeve. 'With the grey hair. There behind the lipstick counter.'

'Who is she?'

'Mmm-hmm-mmhmm ...' Humming casually, turning away, spraying a sampler on the back of her hand, murmuring: 'She's Sloyan. From Tubbercurry. Take care would she see me ...' Walking sideways to the stairs. 'The loveliest girl you ever saw.' Walking properly again upstairs. 'She was going with this fella from Sligo—Jim Troy, a floorwalker in Kellett's, oh a real hard ticket. Waited for him and waited for him, and wouldn't look at another fella. And he had no more notion of marrying than the cat. Wasted her life on him.'

'Did you work in Kellett's?'

'Oh there's Celia. Don't be saying what you're doing. I told her you were working for the *Press*.'

Celia exuded clear language, confidence. My mother was on guard again, silent until the waitress approached. But not the familiar old waitress whose hand she could touch while she ordered. This was a young woman who stood a yard away. My mother's voice dipped—

'What's this quish?'

'Quiche? It's a vegetable omelette on a pastry base.'

'Ah no, love.' Looking up at the waitress' polite shut-door face. Smile: 'I don't know what I want ...'

'Oh God,' Celia said. 'That's what Kevin says.'

'Would you like to come over and look at the counter.' The waitress walked away, my mother followed.

'And what do you say?' I faced Celia.

'What I want.' She took my cool look, gave it back. 'I know what I want.'

Our row began, resumed rather; the same row, continued at each meeting like a conversation, politely sometimes, even with laughter; but the same theme underneath. What was it about? 'It must be nice to be so clear about everything,' I said.

'It is.' More and more openly a row. 'That's why I get my way.'

It was important, whatever it was. Why else was my casually crossed leg shaking? Celia's mouth crimped shut between each remark? Celia and Kevin going to the English rather than the Irish west country had something to do with it. So had sending their children to Protestant rather than Catholic schools. And so had Celia's cars, her housekeepers and the simple pregnant country girls who stayed with her, who minded her children, allowed her to go out when she liked, to attend courses in philosophy, theology. She had left the Catholic Church, weighed it in her steel Scots scales and found it wanting. What had such things in common?

'I'm going to have the soup.' My mother returned. 'They have lovely potato soup you should try, Celia.'

'No. I've ordered, Mrs Kenny.'

They were the opposite of everything my parents did, or didn't do. So obvious. Why hadn't I thought of that before?

'Adrian, what'll you have?'

'I don't feel hungry.'

'Can't you have something. I'm paying.'

'No, I just dropped in to say hello to Celia.'

'Hello.' Celia smiled.

'Goodbye.' Not bad.

She was the opposite of Irish-Catholic, kind-timid, warm-wily Mama. Was that why Kevin had chosen her, why he tolerated, no, relished her extravagance? Was that why I disliked her? But I too was on the run from Mama—so why did I dislike Celia?

—Because you're afraid.

—Of what?

—Of the adult world, freedom. Cut the Irish umbilical cord—isn't that what Barrett said to you years ago?—and you're onto the international line. Clear language. Direct speech. Infinite possibility.

'Yes?'

'Wicklow Harbour, please.'

'Single?'
'Return.'

Down down down again in the mine cage, each descent taking longer; a day, two, sometimes three days now before I was settled in the stillness, the darkness, before I could breathe in that air becoming thinner all the time. More frequent now the split-second headache. Sometimes it was Friday, the week's end, before I grasped the story-line, vanishing like the ragworms down into Wicklow strand when the tide went out; the tantalizing tail-tip I had glimpsed in my last sentence still waving before my eyes as I walked up to the railway station—

'The moon, rolling between clouds no bigger than itself, lighting up the snowflakes bolting into the grass ...'

'Cork.'
  'Sorry?'
'A ticket to Cork!'
'Alright. No need to shout.'
I went to the phone and called Barrett.

He met me at the station. One look at him and the remarks I had been rehearsing on the train crawled away in shame.

  'How are you?' He stood waiting for my answer, his eyes on mine.

  'OK. How are you?'

He began a reply, stopped, ran his fingers through his hair.

  'Will we have a drink?' I said.

  'OK ...' Pause. 'OK.'

Was that an answer to my first as well as my second question? Somehow the game of draughts had begun. Barrett had already jumped me, been crowned and his king was in place, ready to move backwards as well as forwards.

—So what? He's just defending himself.

—Against what?

—You're a swallow hole, sucking everything down.

—He's the swallow hole. If I don't watch out I'll be dragged down into his kingdom.

—Why did you come down here so?

—To learn.

—Learn my eye. You know where you should be—in Dublin with Ruth. You're on the run again.

'We'll try in here.' Barrett eased open a door. 'About the only pub in Cork that hasn't a television.' He went to the counter, his look wiping the smile off the barman's face; then, in the voice of a priest announcing penance after an honest confession, he ordered two pints. He had too the priest's power of reserving speech, falling silent now, cowl thrown up onto his head.

'Good luck,' I said.

Barrett raised his glass, reflected, said a measured 'God bless.'

I broke first. 'I've never had Beamish before.'

Barrett smiled.

'The *vin de pays*,' I said.

Barrett smiled still more. Silence then. Such sad silence. Barrett seemed to be sinking, begging me to lend a hand. I broke again—'Talking of wine, I was reading *The Guardian* in the train on the way down—'

'It's the only paper I can read nowadays without—' Barrett stopped, said a polite 'Sorry?'

'No, I mean it was just this review I was reading, something about Henry James, and it had this story about him drinking Champagne—you know, sitting down in his morning coat, with his top hat upside down on the floor beside him, very grand and deliberate—'

Barrett nodded, leaned closer, like the priest to the confessional grille.

'—I forget who it was. Anyhow, whoever was with him was suddenly hit by the desire to pour some Champagne into James' top hat, because, you see, he couldn't imagine what on earth James would do or say when he put the hat on again. So—'

'You mean—' Barrett's face fell in appalled sadness. 'You mean, somebody actually did that?'

'Well, it wasn't so much a joke as …'

—Oh my God you fool, will you shut up! Don't speak. Let him speak.

Silence.

'Do you know *The Golden Bowl*?' I said.

'I can't read novels.' Barrett began to shake his head, stopped.

I addressed the side of his face. 'I can't write novels. I think it's because I'm asking the wrong questions. You know in the Sherlock Holmes stories …'

—I give up.

'… Holmes says that solving a mystery is just a matter of asking the right questions. Well, the same is true of writing novels, but in writing novels the style is the equivalent of Holmes' questions, and we're so used to reading American, English, French novels that we think their style, their questions are the only ones, and so of course we get the wrong answers.'

'You just have to be like …' Not silent now, now Barrett was interrupting, swimming up out of his swallow hole, the eagle that waited on prey was gliding down from his cliff ledge 'Like W.G. Grace!' Heads turning as his voice rose, as he seized an empty bottle, held it like a cricket bat. 'And when that ball comes down the wicket you have to step out and—' Barrett slogged an almighty six over the boundary.

'Keep it down there, lads!' the barman called.

'What's the ball? Life?'

'Anything! Camels! You've got to step out and … SIX!'

'That'll do now.' The barman plucked the bottle away. 'Drink up there.'

A new moon smiling in the west, Mars burning in the east, a church lit up inside throwing stained-glass light out into the dark as we walked home. All was beautiful. But Barrett was silent again, walking ahead, cowl thrown up again, high priestly forehead tilted to the clouds. I caught up with him; he walked faster. He wanted to be alone. I fell back, but now I seemed to be setting the pace, and Barrett was falling alongside but still not speaking, instead giving me the freezing blast of his silence. What was this? Art? Power? Apples or plums?

'What brings you down here?' Niamh was paler, older.

'I just took a notion.'

She stood aside as Barrett folded his wings and glided silent indoors.

'Treasure that independence.' His voice had an angry sliver. He searched for the bottle opener, his silence menacing as he walked about the small room through children's homework, bills, newspapers. He sat down in his grey overcoat, breathing through his nostrils, looking at the floor. Through the thin wall came the sound of next-door neighbours' laughter. A click! Then the sound of the same laughter.

'They're the strangest people.' Niamh caught at the crumb of conversation before it was swallowed in Barrett's silence. 'They sit there tape-recording themselves and then playing it back.'

Loud laughter then at the sound of their laughter. Another click and they began talking loudly again.

'And then they'll play that back. They're morons!' Barrett stood, glided up suddenly into the room again. 'Is there any'— he fastened his eyes on Niamh—'drink?'

'I left one bottle aside for you for the morning.'

'Where is it?'

'You'll only have a hangover, and then you won't be able to work.'

'I'm OK,' I said chattily.

'Where is it?' Barrett kept his eyes fixed on Niamh.

'You'll only be giving out to me in the morning—'

'I will not have this ... *betrayal.*'

Silence. Then—click!—more play-back conversation from next door, followed by loud laughter.

'I'M GOING IN THERE—!' Barrett made for the door.

'No, don't.' Wearily Niamh stood before him. 'It's no use.'

'If I had a GUN ...!'

'I have the same problem in Wicklow ...'

Barrett looked at me, looked as if he might hit me a crack in the face. Then he was the eagle again, gliding back to his cliff ledge, reaching down a book from a shelf, reading aloud—

> *'I have desired to go*
> *Where springs not fail,*
> *To fields where flies no sharp and sided hail*
> *And a few lilies blow*
>
> *And I have asked to be*
> *Where no storms come,*
> *Where the green swell is in the havens* DUMB!'

His voice rose to a roar, a sudden silence fell next door.

> '—*And out of the swing of the sea.*'

'Hopkins?'

No full-marks smile from Barrett. 'He started this whole thing ...' Talking aloud, he went about the room, stopped suddenly, said meekly 'Can I have that bottle?'

'Take it!' Niamh opened the fridge, drew out a bottle from the back. 'And you can take yourself off too. Go on. Go!' She walked out of the room.

'Hopkins ...' Barrett snapped off the cap, poured himself a brimming glass.

'You should apologize to her.'

'My thinking is way beyond that.' He passed the bottle, eyes fixed on mine, challenging disagreement. The look continued, steady forceful as an arm-wrestler pressing another's arm down to the table. Was everything to do with power? Yes was the answer, as I instinctively withstood Barrett's stare. What was this no-power world, that novel which had me in its power, which I used all my power to keep? A dream of life? a work of art? My gaze pressed against Barrett's gaze. Holding his stare with my own, I took the bottle, filled my glass to the brim.

'Good luck.' His eyes lowered, a smile like sun breaking through mist warmed his woebegone face as I drank the freezing beer.

We talked till dawn.

Apples and plums.

In the train again. Rattled now. Up through Galway, back to Mayo. The earwig shaken from the typewriter, the primate fleeing up the trees from evolution.

'Not you, love?'

One sentence, a breath of turf-fire air, and I was back in that home that was not home, that form worn in the long grass of memory.

'Dada'—so Margaret called my father—'rang to know if you were here.'

'Here I am.'

'Sure you can't spend your life going from place to place.' She set a dish of Irish stew before me, the bottom of the pot, a creamy sediment of potato mutton carrot onion. 'Will I ring and say you're here?'

There was a telephone now in this place which once had been to me a cut-off nether world. A television too, flickering and murmuring like the fire, company in this grey solitude. Margaret minded both with equal care, tuned the picture as deftly as she arranged embers with the long-shanked tongs. 'I hear Petie was in town.'

'Does he not come up to visit?'

'I haven't seen him since Austin's funeral.'

Five years since she had seen her brother, though he lived only five miles away.

'You should go out to visit him.'

'Why would I?' Simple surprise in her voice.

'He's your brother.'

'Brother is right.' She turned to the TV.

Her life was arranged now in this half-lit corner; a full turf barrel at her right hand, teacup and prayerbook to her left; television set beneath the uncurtained window that gave a view to the empty road. I looked with her at the film, a documentary of a North African tribe—long-jawed, blue-hooded folk carrying huge thorny bundles of brushwood on their backs. Beside the television, like a still from the film, stood the painted photo of my great-grandmother—her face fiercened by poverty, hooded by a shawl.

'God, the poor creatures.' Margaret yawned. 'See is there anything good on UTV.'

'I think I'll take a walk.'

'And do.' Margaret settled down to the afternoon movie.

An invalid havened in a corner, but her life flowed on. She could cut a brother out of her life as smartly as she had once pulled weeds. I was the one still rooted in the past.

Here I had been sent by my mother as a boy, back to my father's old home, set free for the summer from their ambition. Here I had been sent to the spring well, stopped to watch a splash snaking down the hot road-tar into the grass verge; stopped next day to spill more, see more. Here the bucket had begun to leak. Here I had gone off the road. Here drop by drop the stalactite had formed.

Memories matted like groundsel carpeted the yard. Why not walk over them as I walked over this pungent weed? Fly from them like the goldfinches. Flow away from them like the water oozing down the cressy bed from the old spring. Walk out the creaking gate—like this—onto the open road. How willingly I would, as soon as I had finished my book. When would I finish my book? As soon as I had walked over these memories matted like the groundsel.

Uneasy strangers in the world they had entered, my parents had held tight to this familiar handrail, the country past they had fled. Their grip had become my grip. I stepped it out along the shinbone of road between wet fields brimming with memories.

In a way this road had been my father's home. At one end of the ridge—the cottage where he had been born, where Petie now lived. At the other end—the house where their mother had settled in middle age, where Margaret sat now.

'People used to say Mother had left Father,' Margaret would explain. 'But they were as happy together as apart.'

'So why live apart?'

'She had got used to living on her own. Father had been away in Lancashire for so long.'

By then their children had grown and gone, except my father. Youngest son, he was made messenger boy, walked these five miles driving a cow, bringing news back and forth; until at fourteen he was apprenticed, and left this hard road forever.

My heels rattled on the hard road. Yes—I was walking out to Petie now, but not to visit, no. Walking this road as if it was any other road, looking straight ahead. And this boreen I was swinging into now, banks swelling with green moss, a storm-thrush silent in the bare ash tree, is like any other boreen—

There he is!

I ducked, and through the thorn hedge watched my uncle hopping down the field, a red plastic basin of seed-oats under one arm, scattering—no, pelting handfuls with broadcast sweeps, each fistful flying from the catch of his wrist that shot seeds into damp brown earth, earth scored deep with teeth marks from the harrow. Power. Force. Life.

[156]

Ape man, I walked bent-double out of sight, catching the scent of earth, a scent so strong I could almost hear it.

—Sssh!

I walked out the boreen again, to the tar road back to the town—but not to Margaret's.

'Dublin, please.'

'Single or—?'

'Single!'

There was no escape.

'Would you like to have dinner with me?'

'I'm visiting my mother.'

'Oh.'

'I could meet you for a drink later.'

'I'll be gone back to Wicklow.'

'Oh.'

'Would you like to visit me down there some day?'

'Yes.'

Down down to that book, the mother of all books; two ... three hundred pages, each page getting thicker, stiffer as I pasted on still more changes.

'He was an oblong handsome man with a red hatchet face; in a green suit ...'

—That's it. But suggest that the hatchet is buried in the green.

'He was an oblong handsome man with a red hatchet face in a deep green suit, about forty years old ...'

There was a knock on the door. I jumped. A sheet of paper fell in a clatter through the silence. She's come—

Jesus! 'Hello, Dada.'

'Yes, I was just out in Stillorgan,' he laid an antique clock, brass-faced, walnut-cased, into my hands; freed, his own hands began to fidget, 'and I just thought I'd drop this down …'

'Ah, you shouldn't have.'

'Ah, I just saw it down in Lionel Jackson's. The best you could say is that it's—kkmm!—serviceable.'

'Still …' Tick tock. TICK. TOCK.

'Well, how's the writing going?'

'OK—will we take a stroll down the pier? There's a ship in from Africa …'

'He was an oblong handsome man with a red hatchet face in a deep green suit, about forty years old. His waistcoat came up to the collar of—'

Ra-tat-ta.

She's come—

'Stephen!'

'How's it going?' He set a bundle of papers on the table— *Rolling Stone, Press, TLS*.

'OK. Will we take a stroll down the pier? There's a ship in from Lagos …'

—His waistcoat came up to the collar of … 'What's news?'

'Helen is coming back to Dublin.'

'Really?'

'She and Jonathan have split up.'

'What happened?'

Stephen shrugged to hide his happiness. 'And did you hear about Jamie?'

—The collar of … of … 'No. What?'

'He went to Greece for a holiday. Ended up in jail.'

'Oh no.'

'Public indecency.'

'What!'

'Stripped off and streaked.'

★

'He was an oblong handsome man with a red hatchet face in a deep green suit, about forty years old, and the waistcoat came up to the collar of ...'

—Ra-ta—

—She's come.

'Hello.'

'Come in.'

She stepped into the tomb womb gloom, looked about. 'This is where you live.'

'This is where I exist.'

She smiled. I said, 'You took the day off?'

'It's a bank holiday.'

Ta-ra-ta-ta!

Damn damn damn damn!

Standing on the doorstep—Katherine and her friend Kate, friends from The Castle; at home only on high stools, in cigarette smoke. What force drove them down to Wicklow that day?

'Stephen was telling us you were here.'

'Come in ...'

'It's too fine. Come on out—we've brought a picnic.'

'I'm with someone.'

'All the better. We bought twice too much. We'll go down to the harbour.'

The harbour. For me now it was like the punishments Greek gods had devised for those who offended.

'Hell,' Katherine said, 'we forgot to bring a corkscrew.'

'I've one in the house.' I went back to fetch it ... ran upstairs to the typewriter—

'He was an oblong handsome man with a red hatchet face in a deep green suit, about forty years old, and the waistcoat came up to the collar of ...'

—The collar of what? God, just give me one word. One—

—His!

' ... the collar of his ...' Thank you, thank you, God!

His his ... I ran back to the harbour. 'Here we are!'

[159]

'Thank God,' Kate said.

The sun stayed out but the stink of rotting shellfish died away; the wine ran out but the talk seemed to last. It was the sort of day you plan for but never get. There was a regatta: boats, yachts, speedboats at play in the harbour, a helicopter demonstrating sea rescue, a plane dipping its wings feet above the waves. A French corvette was in, girls darted about snatching the sailors' caps, the sailors snatched kisses in return. It got hot. Ladybirds flew in swarms. Girls wearing matelot caps walked arm in arm with bare-headed matelots. The harbour's granite arms shimmered in the heat.

'What would Ireland be like if we had weather like this always?' Kate asked.

'Like this,' Katherine said.

There was a carnival too. Katherine won on the roulette table, spent it all in a bar but stood up sober when Kate suggested we drive down to Gorey where another festival was to begin.

Warm dusk when we reached there. As if for the time being their role was played, Katherine and Kate met other friends, fellow citizens of Bohemia, leaving Ruth and me alone to talk.

And I learned—coincidence—that her father came from this town; that his family had been settled there three centuries, since some Williamite forebear landed off some English ship; and since there was daylight still, we walked about the town where she had never been until today—coincidence; and finding an old graveyard, we walked in and there—coincidence—were her family's tombstones, row on row, the same sober sufficiency from the first slate slab with seventeenth-century dates, Old Testament names; and I learned that her father, Benjamin, last of them, penniless, first to leave this place, had gone to Dublin for work; and she told me that this very day was—coincidence—the anniversary of his death.

'How long ago was this?'

'I was fourteen.'

Childhood's end. It seemed to me suddenly that my enormous wilful childhood was coming to an end. Coincidence throbbing out now like the day's heat. Still talking, we strolled hand in hand back through dark warmth to the bar.

Even Bibby, gate-keeper to Tír na nÓg, smiled up from his circle of curly-headed boys as I appeared with this girl. And still talking with, listening to this girl, I learned that her father had not died in Dublin but in England where he had gone, again looking for work; failing to find any, falling down one day ... and so he had died and been buried—where, she didn't know—a stranger in that country from where his forebears had come.

Why did I find so beautiful now her face not glancing back as we drove from Gorey late that night? The ease with which she shrugged off her family's centuries there, her father's death? And yet not shrugged off, for her sallow throat had tensed as she said that this day was the anniversary of his death. How beautiful too, cigarettes stuck in mouth corners, were Katherine's, Kate's instinctive, unquestioning dropping her off at my door, bip-bipping the horn and driving on for Dublin. I thanked The Castle from my heart: for all the smoke I had breathed in its bar, it had the true salt air of freedom.

Instinctively, unquestioningly, we went upstairs, through my bunker back room, past the paper-laden table—

'... and the waistcoat came up to the collar of his ...'

—into the bedroom; footsteps so silent on the three-inch newspaper underlay, breath so loud in the double-glazed stillness, clothes falling in crashes. How slowly then we moved towards each other, yet how steadily, easily in the pitch-dark silence; and as we met, so deeply, fiercely, peacefully met, through all the soundproofing came the blare of the horn of the French corvette sailing out of the harbour below, full tide carrying her over the sand bar ... and just then I entered her; and—a cry of pain, for she was virgin—she smile-whispered '...' and I knew then that we would be together always somehow; and then it was my turn to cry. I got up and drew back the thick-lined curtains, slid back the double-glazing, let down the window sash, lay down in bed again alongside her; and together, listening to the beautiful clangor carried in by the sea wind, we fell asleep in each other's arms, her hand still closed on my handkerchief red with her blood.

JAMIE

– 11 –

Green engine, new amber carriages: the Wicklow train wound
screeching into Westland Row, the same station I used to arrive
in from Mayo as a boy. Walking down the old ramp, case in one
hand and typewriter in the other, I remembered the light-headed
feeling of seeing the city traffic again; my brother Noel's face,
brown after a country summer, pale as our father revved the car.

—What happened the Zephyr?

—I got rid of that.

—What's this?

—A Rover.

A Rover was different. It was the same as any other car, but
bigger stronger. Like me now. A virgin no more. Memories
parted like the breezy air I strode through. Nassau Street,
Dawson Street—

'Can I meet you? Tonight?' Voice a little high.

'I'm seeing someone.'

'Your mother?'

She shook her head, turned to a call from down the shop—

'Crudens?' A parson, not moving, stood waiting to be served.
This was a Protestant bookshop for Protestant people. Some
priests in Gill's had the same manner, children in sweetshops too.

'Where are you staying?' She returned, placid. 'At home?'

'A friend's house. He's away for a year. I'm minding his cat.'

A cramped house. It looked as if it had been built not so much for living in as to bring the crescent to a Georgian conclusion. Two hinge sockets in the granite cornerstones suggested it had been a gatekeeper's lodge. Another gate-lodge, but not in Westmeath. Another low-ceilinged place, not the Brazen Head. Another small terraced house, not in Wicklow Harbour. Slowly I was advancing on my father's mansion.

I pushed open the door. A stink of cat. Two tiny triangle rooms, one above the other like a sandwich. I looked around—books, books. Allan had come to Ireland to study Eng. Lit.

Empty bottles, manuscripts. He had drifted into the literary pub scene. Theodolite, boots. He had drifted off the scene, taught himself surveying, and now he had a job in West Africa. Anything was possible. Anything.

A neurotic miaou, a Siamese cat came down the slat stairs, arched against my shins, nosed at food and flickered back upstairs. I set the typewiter on Allan's chest of drawers. The hero was back in town.

Ten o'clock, a knock on the door.

'You met your someone?'

'Yes.'

'Can I ask who?'

'He's a priest.'

'Not a parson?'

No smile. 'I'm taking instruction. I want to become a Catholic.'

'Why?'

'I've always wanted to.'

'Why didn't you?'

'I think out of loyalty to my father's memory.'

'And why now? Nothing to do with me, I hope. Because—'
Voice a little high again.

She shook her head.

Silence. She sat still, one long brown hand upon the other.

'Who's this priest?'

'Father Hyde. He's an old man.'

'Not a Jesuit?'

Nod.

I had heard of him at school, stories of his few words. One story told how, for a bet, two scholastics entered his room resolved not to speak until Fr Hyde had broken, spoken. So they had entered his silence which lasted for half an hour, an hour ... until there was another knock on the door, when Fr Hyde smiled and finally spoke—'I'm afraid we've been interrupted.'

'What does he talk about?'

'He answers my questions.'

'What are they?'

'He asks me to read a chapter of the Gospel, and the next week asks me if I understand it.'

'And do you?'

'Yes. I'm a Christian.'

'So why become a Catholic?'

'I told you. I feel at home there.'

'That's why I can't stand it.'

'What's wrong with that?'

'There's more to life than home,' I said.

'Exactly.'

Silence.

I looked at her, her eyes shut. I tried the Fr Hyde approach, shut my own eyes. More silence. This time she spoke—

'I didn't have a home.'

'What did you have?'

'Mayhem.'

'*Par exemple?*' The urbane approach.

For example: having breakfast tea from jamjars because her

mother had smashed the china; sitting on orange crates because her mother had given away, thrown out, smashed or sold the furniture, dealers having discovered that place where a Regency table, a Victorian chair, remnants of old prosperity, could be bought from a raging lady—that Horse Protestant face I remembered—for a few shillings; raging regret then—mother smashing malacca cane on daughter's back; mother going to bed for a week, a month and sending daughter to an orphanage; mother miaouing like a cat outside daughter's door to prevent her from studying; mother locking daughter into bedroom for a week to starve her; daughter waking at night to find mother holding a knife to her throat; mother kicking daughter between the legs, declaring, You'll never have children now! Mother breaking down ...

'... And then I got her into hospital.'

A one-minute précis.

'You'd have been better off dead.'

'Sometimes I think I am.' She shut her eyes again, dark-lidded. I shut mine, thought of all that happening a hundred yards from my happy home. Was that contrast the reason for this sympathy? Or was it that there was no contrast at all? But how could that be? No rows in our home—never. No answering back—ever. I opened my eyes. Midnight already. How had two hours gone?

She stood. 'I have to go.'

'I'll walk with you.'

'I've moved.'

'You too. Where?'

'Percy Place.'

'That's posh.'

'It's a flat. I'm sharing.'

'Who with?'

'A friend. She works with me.'

Something in her look, her smile reminded me of Esther—Esther back in New England now with a woman lover. 'Do you love women?'

'I love you.'

'I love you,' I echoed. Three words I had never put in that order before.

We walked the canal bank in silence between the water and the trees. Why had I said 'I love you'? That account of her upbringing producing mere pity? The mention of her turning Catholic bringing out tribe loyalty? Or simply herself? What was herself?

'Have you ever slept with a woman?' Voice a little higher.

'Yes.'

Yea.

'I was only sixteen. I just lay on her breast. That's all I wanted.'

'What did she want?'

'I used to work in a chemist's. She used to come into the shop, the others said she was—you know ...' Timid.

'Lesbian. You know the word—say it.'

'So I went down to her house one day'—not timid—'and knocked on her door and—'

'She took you in.'

'Maybe I just wanted a big Mama.'

'Have you ever slept with a man?'

'You.'

'Only? I thought you'd have had more offers.' Blasé.

'Why?'

'You're beautiful.'

'My mother told me I was ugly as sin.' She crossed Leeson Street. I held her brown hand.

'How could you believe that?'

'She said I was yellow. I used to put peroxide in the bath to make my skin white.'

'Helen, a friend of mine, looked into your shop the other day. She said that you were "absolutely gorgeous".'

'The first time a man asked me to go to bed with him, I didn't know what he meant. "Why?" I said. I thought he was tired.' She smiled at my smile. 'Have you ever slept with a man?'

'No.'

'You want to?'

[169]

'I don't know.'

'You're very frightened of all that?'

'Is it that obvious?'

We passed Huband Bridge, her answer drowned by the waterfall roar. She stopped before a double flight of steps leading to twin hall doors. 'Here I am.'

'Which one is yours?'

'Thirty-seven.'

I looked at its comrade. 39 Percy Place … Where had I seen that address before? On my birth certificate. I stared at the house I could not remember. 'I was born here.' Coincidence. Curtains parted, a girl's face looked out.

'I'd better go.' She drew back as I kissed her cheek.

The mile walk had passed like a hundred yards. The walk back—even with the warmth of 'I love you', with yet another of those coincidences whispering like the poplar leaves—became an ordinary mile again.

Back with the cat, I sat down to write. To finish the bloody book. Only then would I be free to be with her. Why? And why did my hero resist, clinging like a limpet to the rock of vagueness? The cat slipped like a shadow from the bed and onto my lap, shivering as she slept, warming my knees as I laboured. Rain was clicking on the window. Fat drops, amber in the old green question-mark street-light, slid down the pane. All at once I put down my pen.

—Why not stop writing for a change, close the book on this family business?

I closed the manuscript.

—And put it away.

I put it in Allan's dressing-table drawer.

—And see what happens.

I shut the drawer—screech—and sat listening to the rain shooting from the downpipe, rushing down the shore outside.

The cat shivered as if naked and sank deeper into my lap.

– 12 –

The top window sash screeched open, Stephen's head appeared and down dropped the key in the same old sock. The same brown hall, the envelopes withering on the table, the postcard from Rome still unclaimed; the same view of a hundred chimney pots from the landing window. All as it had been when I first climbed these stairs four years before.

'So ...' Stephen lying back again in the sitting-room dusk, blowing smoke rings that drifted like Van Morrison's song—

'The love that loves to love to
Say goodbye to Madame George ...'

Helen back too, sitting opposite him. Standing to peck my cheek, then pit-pat stocking-footed to the kitchen, where the old gas oven still roared out heat.

'Well, young Kenny.' Stephen, eyes willing me to go away, smiled, 'You're back.'

Everything the same—holy smoke! Helen's blue silk dress still on the back of his bedroom chair—but none of us the same. Helen was thirty now, thistledown settling; but not settling with Stephen, not here where the fire was lit, hearth swept and curtains drawn shut—it reminded me of the Wicklow house I had fled. Now it was Stephen who was clinging to a dream of home.

'Here.' Helen returned with beer-glasses of wine.

Stephen's eyes followed her in a feast of pride, love possession, willing her to sit down again. She didn't. He drained his glass, willing me to finish mine. I drank up and he said, 'So, where are you off to?'

'Into town.'

'I'll be with you.'

Helen went into her bedroom. Through the doorway I glimpsed its tidiness—Stephen's preparations for her homecoming—dissolve a little more. Swssh of skirt thrown down, clatter of boots on the floor.

Wearily he stood before the fire, looked at his father's memoriam card photo on the mantel as he listened to the last of the record—

'The love that loves to love to
Say goodbye to Madame George ...'

—before lifting the needle.

'Where'll we go?' Helen wore the same expensive perfume she had that night I first saw her with Stephen in Synnott's.

'Synnott's?' Stephen said.

'How about The Bailey?'

The traffic seemed loud, the lights bright. Because I was new back in town? My stomach was tense. Because I had no novel to hide in now? Police everywhere. Because the British ambassador had been murdered? Stephen linked Helen's arm as we entered the bar.

'Jamie.'

Jamie too was as I had first seen him, standing at the counter, toe on rail, chatting with someone. Calm, but with the glow of elation. It reminded me of smouldering straw, the dull rose glow that needs only a breath to make it blaze again.

'Here we are again.' Still wearing his oatmeal sportscoat, middle button fastened, his hair in the same fifties parting, conversation as straight. 'I'm sorry, do you know Denis? Denis is an actor.'

Denis turned: young, florid, drunk, an American voice. 'Helen, what'll you have?'

'You.' Helen laughed.

'On the rocks?'

'Anywhere.'

She must have met Denis before, maybe even had arranged to meet him there, but that was the first night I saw them together, and realized that already, again, she had slipped through Stephen's fingers. In five minutes, in the easy ruthless way of lovers, she and Denis had elbow-slid a few yards down the counter to be alone.

This was the world I had glimpsed between double-doors: peasants' children set loose in the city. This was the world I had wanted to enter but had held back from and instead sat hatching my china egg in the straw. I would have been brooding still on that dead perfection if I hadn't met Ruth. So why wasn't I with her tonight?

Stephen, as if asking himself some similar question, looked blankly at an *Evening Press* on the counter, open at a half-page photo of the British ambassador's car, the bomb-cratered road. From down the counter came Helen's bubbling laughter. Stephen turned the page, looked at Ewart-Biggs' photo—a stage diplomat in monocle and morning coat.

'Bastards,' he said.

'Sorry?' Denis glanced over his shoulder.

'Fucking IRA.'

'Maybe he deserved it.'

'Deserved to lose his life?' Stephen's voice rose. 'Who decides that?'

Denis shrugged and turned back to Helen, absorbed in drawing a lemon pip from her gin.

'Not me.' Jamie raised his glass.

Stephen walked out with the peculiar dignity of the defeated. Helen watched him through the window. Denis looked at her.

'Just my luck'—she was murmuring to me; a few hours had passed, she was taking her last drink in a swallow—'to fall for an *actor*.'

Denis took her arm and they went out the swing door.

'He looked around and now he's found.' Jamie rested elbow on counter, chin on hand, cigarette between lips, eyes downcast: smouldering straw.

Ruthless, I breathed on it. I wanted a blaze to shatter that china egg. 'Are you going on anywhere?'

'There's a club just opened.'

'I might go with you.'

'Do.' Jamie breathed out in a sudden smile and the tip of his cigarette glowed.

Broken steps down to a flooded basement area, a door floating on a blocked drain's sewage—Charon's raft to the Elysian Fields. No light except a peephole's pinpoint. It vanished, there was a rattle of locks, the door opened. I followed Jamie inside. Up there out of sight lay the white china egg. Down here it was dark. With the grace of the world-weary Jamie threaded a way to shoots of candle flame. A bar appeared. In a minute he was again leaning elbow on counter, chin propped on hand.

'What'll it be?'

'Let me.' He shook out money, began to count, gave up and pushed it all across the counter. 'Have you a Campari?'

The boy behind the counter pronounced, 'I *am* a Campari.'

'And soda am I.' Jamie was chuckling, in his world again. He crossed the floor to the Gents, returned a minute later, bald spot combed over; paused and mimed like a boxer's left-right a moment's furious dancing, greeted a couple of middle-aged men in suits waltzing cheek to check, came to rest once more, elbow on counter, hand propping chin; pronounced—'Fruits in suits.'

'Who are they?'

'A pair of eejits.'

'Why?'

'I can't stand that Darby and Joan stuff.'

'Maybe they like each other?'

'I wouldn't be surprised.' He touched his wrist, fingering, I thought at first, a scar there—its stitch weals like a zip; in fact catching a thread unravelled from his cuff, nipping it off neatly.

'Want to dance, Jamie?'

'Na.'

'Why do you come here?'

'I like it.' He shut his eyes.

I looked around—gloom growing into yellow light. A boy, red-speckled with desperate acne, was riding another boy pig-gyback, both squawking the words of the song—

'Friday night and the lights are low
Looking out for a place to go ...'

Two bushy-bearded men sunk in a beanbag were groping one another.

' ... You're in the mood for dance
And when you get the chance
You are the dancing queen.'

'Like what?'

Jamie looked up as another song began. 'This is nice though. Will we dance?' Singing tunelessly along, he steered out onto the floor; weary-youthful, movement cut to essentials, an old sailor pushing the boat out once more.

'Don't cry for me, Argentina
The truth is I never left you ...'

Gliding past two trim young men—

'This is the sort of thing'—one turned to the other—'makes me wonder why I ever come back to Ireland.'

'And as for fortune ...' Jamie went on singing. His indifference was catching. The two were laughing openly at him, at me too as I joined in—

'*And as for fame …*'

Jamie's face was glowing now, burning straw. I felt my eyes sting with—surprise, surprise—tears of tension released. Through them I saw one of the bearded men put a hand in the other's trouser flies. The spotted boy was lashing his mount's flank, making him caper about the room. Blue sparks fizzed from a broken switch, lighting up the cellar ceiling, an exact Georgian curve.

' … *I chose free-dom …*'

Eyes closed, Jamie sang, ran out of words, went on lilting—

'Lalala—lalala—lalala …'

'La-la.' I put my arms about him. He slipped away like smoke, back to the counter.

'Are you alright?'

'I'm puffed.'

'Want to go?' I asked, hopeful. I had done my bit for Ireland. Now I wanted to flee.

'What do you want to do?'

What did *I* want to do? How on earth would I know?

Jamie nodded—'How about that chicken?'—and watched me take first steps across the floor.

'Like to dance?'

'OK.'

Dancing with a boy, a scarf of yellow silk loose about his neck, tight-trousered balls pressed to mine, I felt a stir, froze, pressed back and felt my cock stir; panicked as I had in Connemara long ago when my father, teaching me to swim, took his hand from under my stomach and let me float in the green Atlantic. I wasn't sinking. I was floating.

'What's your name?'

'Al.'

'Al!'

'One sec …' He drifted, fast, over to another boy.

Afloat in the sea now, able to swim now, damn well going to swim now, swim out to Crump Island now. '… Would you like to dance?'

'Sank you. I am Helmut.'

German. Not exactly nice now. Fingertips growing bold with my behind, a yoke like a car jack shoving up between my thighs. I raised the standard with light conversation—

'And what are you doing in Ireland, Helmut?'

'I am doing postgraduate research.'

'I see. On what?'

'Shelley.'

'Really—'

Conversation stopped, a rough-grained tongue shoved between my lips. Tongue, prick, fingertips losing interest as the music stopped. 'Sank you.'

I spiralled across the floor. 'Al!'

His breath dope-scented, chapped lips brushing mine, drawing away ... he rambled off again. Tingling, I waded back to land.

'Jamie, what'll you have?' Champagne! Brandy! Brandyand-champagne!

'I'm OK'—looking up—'Al.'

'Jamie—me old flower.' Al swayed past.

'Do you know him?'

'He stayed with me one summer.' Jamie still held the loose thread from his sleeve, rolling it absently between finger and thumb. 'He's trouble.'

Great.

'Al, would you like to ...?'

'No thanks.'

That cool frown. Why was it so familiar? I placed it as I went creeping back to the bar. The Sacred Heart girl's look when you pushed your luck, asked for a second dance, a date. I felt it appear on my own face when, as the last dance came, Helmut made a round of the floor, ending up in despair before me—

'Vant to—?'

'No thanks.'

'Will we go?' Jamie withdrew the hand that propped his chin.

'Where?' I breathed again.

'The Manhattan should be open now.' Glow.

Walking with Jamie down moonlit O'Connell Street, I saw a woman walk before us, in her hand a red-stamped bag from one of my father's shops. *Kennys Shoes* winking before me as we passed the GPO, crossed the Liffey, following my father's shoes, shoes I would not step into. Lest it mean shoving him out of them? Lest I no longer be that father's son?

Cold thoughts to carry home from a gay nightclub. *Kennys Shoes* turned left at the Green, we turned right. Omen omen—I gnawed at its meaning as we walked to Kelly's Corner.

'You're very quiet.' Jamie spoke.

'What's this?'

'A coffee bar.'

A door between derelict shops, the window bricked up. Inside, a coffee urn made steam thick as the white glass mugs.

'What's the attraction?'

'The flesh.'

Half-a-dozen boys, as many men. Tired eyes sparkling, Jamie watched a carrot-headed boy shove a hand down into a tight jeans pocket; looked away as the boy drew out mere cash. Eyes tired again, Jamie rested chin on hand, elbow on counter. Weary, winding down, cheek-skin withering to the coarse grain of middle age; but wouldn't rest, couldn't. Glow, fade, glow like the ash on the cigarette he breathed in and out. Tapping small trim fingernails on the beautyboard—

'Jaca negra, luna grande,
y aceitunas en mi alforja ...'

I took over—

'Aunque sepa los caminos
yo nunca llegaré a Córdoba.'

'You know Lorca?' Doctor's voice.

'Just that one. We read it at school.'

Voice lowering. 'I picked up this kid in Barcelona once. Went back to his place. Turned out next morning it was his home. His old man just said, 'What way did you lie?' A fucking policeman too ... *Córdoba* ...' Tap-tap.

' ... *Lejana y sola.*'

'Do you know Spain?' Passing me a cigarette.

'No. I've an aunt there, a nun.'

'Yeh? What order?'

'Don't know.'

'I tried it for a year myself. The Holy Ghost.'

'What was that like?'

'Loved it. Just wasn't able for the old celibacy. I used to meet this guy behind the high altar at night. You know—after Benediction.'

'Jamie,' Voice rising, 'did you ever love anyone?'

'I did.'

'What happened?'

'Nothing. I was only fourteen.'

'Jamie, I love someone. I think.'

'Yeh?' Striking a match. 'Boy or girl?'

'Ruth.'

'Where's she tonight?' Unsteady hand passing me the light.

'I don't know.' Cigarette shaking in my lips.

'*Por el llano, por el viento* ...' Tap-tap.

' ... *jaca negra, luna roja* ...' Puff puff.

Glow. 'Maybe we'll head off somewhere together. Morocco?'

'OK. I'm not doing anything. You see I've stopped writing my novel ...'

'Start in Spain, get a ferry from Algeciras—'

'—In fact, Jamie, I had to stop writing my novel—' Voice rising.

'—Cross over to Tangiers—' Glow growing.

'You see I've got this character—' Hand trembling.

'—Pick up a couple of tangerines.' Jamie cracked his mug suddenly down on the beautyboard. 'Will we go?'

'Now?'

'Yes!' Doctor's voice—'This coffee's terrible.'

'Jamie—' Following him as he headed out the door.

'Do you have any money?' Hand raised, walking fast to the corner, breaking into a sudden run as a taxi appeared, jumping from the kerb as if from Algeciras pier.

'I've a couple of hundred—'

Jamie pulled open the taxi door—'How much to Rathmines?'

'Hey!' A voice from the door. 'You and your gay-type friend!'

'Did you not pay?'

Jamie jumped into the taxi. 'Keep it for Tangiers.' Feeling for his cigarettes again. 'You know, there's a lot of nonsense talked about paying for sex.' Feeling for matches. 'Some of the loveliest boys...' Striking a light. 'The most beautiful moments of my life ...'

The driver pulled up sharp. 'Look, get out of my fucking car!'

'We don't want to stay in your fucking car!' Jamie jumped out.

'And that'll be seventy p.'

Jamie slammed the door.

'*Ay qué camino tan largo!*'

'*Ay mi jaca valerosa!*'

Oatmeal sportscoat flapping open as he rode to Córdoba, we walked up the Rathmines Road together.

'Aceitunas—that's the word for olives. The Arabs say zeytin—do you think it's the same word?'

'Ceitun ... zeytin ...'

'Could be.'

'Through the Moors ...?' We stopped at the corner of Richmond Hill. Jamie's bald spot shone under the moonlight.

Straight, gay ... mad, sane: with Jamie at my side, frightening differences drew together—like ceitun and zeytin, like the

glow and fade of his cigarette. I clung to him as my china egg
cracked, he clung to me as his youth melted away.

Those were the days of long nights, suddenly dawn as the
streetlamps went out, blackbird song and the clink of milkbot-
tles, the grating of paper as I pushed my door open on yesterday's post.

Only a fat white envelope this morning, hand-delivered.
'Sorry I missed you ...' in my father's swift writing, wrapped
about—no need to ask—a fold of banknotes.

Oh father, father.

Miaou. The cat appeared like a shadow, brushed her side along
my shins and we went up the slat stairs together. I opened
Allan's drawer, looked in at my novel's hero, still there asleep in
his shell ... and quickly shut the drawer again—screech.

— 13 —

I was *living* my novel. That was better than writing it, wasn't it?
Heh? Heh?

There was a lot of dialogue in that walking talking living
novel.

Together, my novel and I walked-talked up to Ashton's Bar
by the Dodder in the evening, finished a chapter over a couple
of pints—one each. We were walking back one night under the
old Ranelagh bridge, listening to the blackbirds still screeching,
when I saw—

Ruth!

—walking past me as if she was deaf. I realized I hadn't
spoken aloud.

'Ruth!'

She stopped. She was holding a white envelope.

'I'm sorry,' I said, 'I've been out of touch.'

'I ask for nothing. You give me nothing.'

'No wonder your mother beat shit out of you. You ask for it.'

'I never asked for that.'

'Why the hell don't you stand up for yourself.'

'I refuse to fight.'

'Then you might as well be dead.'

'I told you. Sometimes I think I am.'

'And that's why you're becoming a Catholic.'

'Christ said He came that we might have life.'

'Jesus! Why don't you go and live with Christ?'

My hero screech-hopped on my shoulder like the blackbirds.

'I'd rather be with you than with Jesus Christ Himself.' Her face was darkened by the dusk. 'Is that a terrible thing to say?'

Were other love affairs like this? Was this a love affair? What were the other couples passing under the bridge saying to each other?

'When are you turning Catholic?'

'The twenty-first of June.'

'The Feast of St Aloysius Gonzaga.' I smiled.

She said, 'You have a cruel mouth.'

'I love you.'

'I have to go.' She fingered the white envelope

'Where to?'

'To a funeral.'

'Who died?'

'A friend.'

'Who?'

'A Mr Hassett.'

A Mr Hassett ... A Mister has it ... A mystery asset ... Bending the line, writhing back into my novel, I made my way home.

Without my daily blood transfusion, the written novel was dying. Each time I looked in on the fat white typescript it seemed more lifeless, remote, unreal. Without that daily loss of blood, I felt more alive, energy shooting through me—up, down. Some of it tapped off into scribbled diary—

'20 NOVEMBER 1976. Opera with Jamie ... 'Jamie. We're still going to Morocco?'

[183]

'Can't. The old lady's got my passport.'

'We can go somewhere else. London?' Blow.

'Na.' Glow. '*Madame Butterfly* is on at the Gaiety though.'

'OK!'

'Are you OK for dough?' Dipping into jacket pocket. 'Here—' Handing me some church porch holy picture: the Virgin Mary standing on a hoop of seven gold stars afloat in a baby-blue sky.

'Jamie, are you alright?'

I didn't care. I was Dante clinging to my Virgil in the underworld. Glow growing, straw crackling, we walked to the theatre.

'Where'll we sit?'

'The gods will do.' Glow fade glow went his cigarette as we climbed the theatre stairs. 'Fucking peasants'—a poster photo of Jack Cruise in amadhaun check cap quickening his step.

The opera had begun, sweet Italian canary song. In his seat, Jamie breathed through lips parted on an imaginary cigarette, eyes closed throughout, free in his ideal world. I looked down. And saw Ruth sitting far below: dark hair cut short, long brown hands composed one upon the other. I longed to call down, but couldn't. Not yet.

Disaffected from his upbringing but so marked by it that he could not change, Jamie was condemned to a life of flight and return. Here he was at rest. Here young and middle-aged Jamie, poet and Doctor Jamie, religious and rebel Jamie, calm and elated Jamie were all at peace together for two hours.

He opened his eyes. 'I like a little saccharine,' his only comment as the curtain came down.

'What'll we have?' Stopping short as he passed the bar. 'Large gin, please.' Knocking it back, the naked Irishman again, no civic skin on his emotions. Maybe not wanting such a skin.

'Thank God the Romans never got to Ireland,' he had remarked one day.

'Why?'

'It's more interesting this way.'

Huskily warbling a bar from *Butterfly*, he turned to the counter. 'Same again.'

Barman: 'You've had enough.'

Doctor Jamie: 'I'll tell you when I've had enough.'

He returned to *Butterfly*. 'They say it's autobiography. Didn't his maid commit suicide?'

'I don't know.' I fluttered back, forth, smiling agreeably to the barman, to Jamie.

'*I don't know. I don't know.* What *do* you fucking know?' His voice rose. Heads turned to the scene.

One, a girl about eighteen, small and pretty, proudly wearing stage make-up still, approached, addressed Jamie.

'I know you.'

Jamie looked at her bright face. 'Were you—?'

She interrupted with a blasé nod, and, in the voice of one artiste addressing another, said, 'You live on Palmerston Road?'

'I did.'

She seemed as fascinated by Jamie as he by her. For her, Jamie was an opera character, his scandalous roles heard of in murmured asides by her parents, perhaps pointed out by a friend who had told her more. 'Where do you live now?'

Jamie answered, asked her name.

'Kathleen Quirke.'

'You must be very talented.'

'I've only a walk-on part.'

'Still,' Jamie insisted. '*Butterfly.*'

She shrugged the corners of rouged lips.

'What do you think of it?' Glow.

'It's alright up on a stage,' Kathleen said.

'How do you mean?' Fade.

'So long as you remember it's not real.'

Jamie turned abruptly away, ordered another drink, murmuring to himself, 'Giacomo Puccini …'

'I know you too.' Kathleen's lips parted in a smile for me—me dusted by gilt from Jamie's wings. As we talked I placed her in the small wood of leafy roads about my home, in the way I had placed Jamie several years before in The Castle, recognized him as the boy who stood at the 12 bus stop, always a little apart. Again he was apart, emptying his glass suddenly, saying, 'I think I'll head off' in that *I do as I like* tone, which tonight left me alone with Kathleen.

As she watched him exit—small, cock-robin-chested, shoulders sprinkled with dandruff, bald spot shining—I saw that she was as disappointed by this real Jamie as he had been by her.

'He's odd.' She turned to me.

Well I remembered it—the Sacred Heart girl's tone of cut-glass commonsense.

'What does he do?'

'He's a doctor.'

When she had laughed, she said, 'What do you do?'

I knew what to say. 'I'm a writer.'

And she smiled the gaze of admiration that she had earlier shone upon Jamie.

24 NOVEMBER. Kathleen called …
When I opened the door, night fog filled that small triangular living-room. Outside, Kathleen was chaining her bike to the lamppost. Stage make-up removed, she was still younger, a sixteen- or seventeen-year-old girl in pink leg-warmers, putting her bike lamp on the table, sitting on the wicker couch. I shifted the cat and sat beside her. Rathmines Town Hall clock struck eleven.

An hour later, we were still kissing, looking into each other's eyes. Her neck and breasts were rose red, she smelled of musk rose.

'Would you like a little mistress?'

'You mean you?'

'Yes, me.'

'Would you like to go upstairs?'

Her face turned serious as we went up the slat stairs.

'You are an artist, aren't you?'

'I am.'

'What are you working on?'

'A novel.'

She looked at the typewriter on the bare chest of drawers.

'I keep it in a drawer,' I murmured.

'I see,' she said uneasily.

'Look—'

Screech! I opened the drawer an inch, peeped inside at the white manuscript. 'You see—' I shut the drawer with a slam I hadn't intended.

Kathleen stepped back, fastened her shirt buttons.

'I'm sorry ...'

'It doesn't matter.'

'Will I see you again?'

She led the way quickly downstairs. 'If you really want to.'

A few really want to.

Is your eel Yvonne too.

'Bye-ee.' She was going out the door, fast.

15 DECEMBER. Kathleen called again ...

'You're early.'

'The opera's closed.'

'Come in.'

She stood on the doorstep. 'I thought we might go out.'

'I have to meet someone.'

She smiled. 'Who?'

'Remember Jamie? Would you like to come too?'

Jamie was waiting in the bar, looking at the mirror behind the counter, absorbed as if it was the opera; dressed with that special

[187]

bad taste you see sometimes in the single-minded—fawn suit, tan shoes, a gold ring set with a diamond chip on his little finger.

'You remember Kathleen.'

'Kathleen.' He shook hands with me.

Not mad. Abstracted. A film of sweat shining from a thousand pores in his face; standing, one foot tensed before the other, as if about to jump a stream. I nudged him—'What'll you have?'

'Em—' Jamie hesitated at the brink. Behind him—twenty years of flight, a thousand boys in a thousand different beds; danger, pleasure, excitement and movement. Youth. 'A Jameson,' he said.

Then he was silent until closing-time, when he said, 'Would you like to come home for a cup of tea?'

'Alright.'

We got the last bus, Kathleen and I sitting together; Jamie in front looking straight ahead, scanning the faces coming on board at each stop: young faces returning from pubs, the pictures ... more young faces—firm cheeks, rich hair, bright eyes, smooth skin dusted with youth-bloom—a stream of youth filling the aisle. James wiped the sweat from his forehead.

We walked up Cowper Road together, Jamie absorbed now, forgetting his invitation, saying 'Night' as we came to my parents' gate and then flicking away his cigarette end so it buzzed through the dark, a red streak hitting the ground as he vanished around the corner.

'He's just ...' Kathleen frowned '... weird.'

'We could go to my parents' house,' I said.

So, through Jamie again, came another first in my life. At the age of thirty-one I brought a girlfriend home.

Kathleen sat on the chaise longue, small legs crossed, one tiny toe resting on my mother's lime-green pouffe, her petite nose wrinkling with distaste as she looked about our family den. Through her eyes I regarded the rusticated fireplace, the crenellation of photos above, the grey cloth donkey—creels full of real turf crumbs from the west—propped against the ormolu clock.

'Oh, sorry—' My mother came in, looking for the newspaper, a pretext to linger. The silence drove her out. But through the double-doors I heard her, a mouse behind skirting-boards, rustle about the dining room, listening. The cup slipped in my sweating fingers.

'Relax, you're an adult, you know.' Kathleen dabbed tea from my tie.

'I'm going to bed now.' My mother's head appeared again.

No visit to Bartley Dunne's alone, to gay disco with Jamie, no German tongue shoved down my throat matched this dread. I said, 'Goodnight.'

'Goodnight,' Kathleen added coldly.

Like the Baily lighthouse three-second beam, my mother's gaze filled the room as she looked at Kathleen, at me. I was destroying the home in my head, wiping out that warm vague gentle spot, I knew, as my stare reflected the beam back upon her. As if blinded by the light, she withdrew.

But in her bedroom overhead, the floorboards creaked as she moved about still. I heard my father murmur.

'Will we go?' I said.

Kathleen sipped her tea deliberately and looked at our Fergus O'Ryan original. 'There's not much *culture*, is there?' She looked at me. 'You had to make your own culture, hadn't you?' She embraced me suddenly.

Kissing her, my mouth was dry, dry as culture.

Creak-creak went the floorboards overhead.

'I could really go for you, you know,' Kathleen said. 'In a big way.'

So why was I walking quickly, very quickly now, down Westland Row?

'Where to?'

'Em … Ballyhaunis.'
'Single or return?'
'Single. No—return!'
Single Nora turn.
Sing gal no return.

'You're down again.'

'John Patrick!'

'Jump in. I'll give you a lift up.'

I got up into the lorry cab. Familiar fields floated below the big windscreen. 'Where are you going?'

'Galway.' He drove a brewery lorry now.

'I'll be with you.'

'Are you not stopping with Margaret?'

'Not today.'

I saw her sitting at the window looking out. The long lorry rumbled past, setting her hedge ashake. We roared vibrating over the fishback hill. I grasped at the past. 'How's John Edward?'

'He's back in England.' John Patrick put his foot down and we swept along between high ditches, a hundred beer kegs rattling behind like my thoughts.

'Are you going through Milltown?' Are you going through my ill town?

'I am.'

How big his hands were, how red his face. I touched my own face, shocked to feel warm flesh there.

'What's bringing you up to Milltown?'

'Em—' One last bolt-hole to hide in, to close. 'That's where my mother came from.'

The nervous look left his face. 'Who's this she was?'

'McNicholas.'

'Sure that's right. Jesus, they've a mighty holding of land up there.'

[190]

After ten years driving this road he knew all on it, gossiping with barmen as he slung full kegs from the lorry, tossing up empties as if they were biscuit tins; lowering a free pint in three gulps and having two more while I finished my first; then back into the cab.

'Look at the wellingtons on him.' He swung past an old man. 'He must be going down for a pint.'

'Who is he?'

'He's Glavey. The bladder's gone. They won't serve him unless he's wearing the wellingtons.'

'Really!'

This was what I wanted, what was bringing me to Milltown—reality's stones to break the dream country that had become my nightmare country; to tear to shreds this country-past cobweb my mother had spun, that I had hung about myself; to walk through it, as you walked through gossamer on autumn mornings. Celia was right—it was a spider's web. It was death.

'Here we are.'

There it was at last, the foot of the rainbow, my mother's old home.

From here she drew the stuff to spin her memories. How her father bound a hen's broken leg with herbs whose names she remembered only in Irish; but she kept no photo of him. How no man could break a horse to harness as he could; but she had got hitched to my father a week after his funeral. Her mother's memoriam card photo was blurred red with her lipstick kisses, but she never returned to this place, the country neighbours of her memories were never invited to her city home.

Now I had returned. Moi! To melt this myth. Jumping down drunk from the cab—its engine-roar, beer-keg rattle bringing neighbours' heads to windows and doors—I walked up to the drab house where dreams were locked.

Bip-ip! John Patrick drove away, lorry-sides ripping branches from the hedges.

The door opened, I entered an ordinary turf-fire kitchen. A gun on the chimney-breast, a collie on the hearth-stone.

'Hello!' Including uncle, aunt, cousins in my brilliant smile. Melt it down! Melt it down!

Insisted on helping. Filled the sheep's trough from the river, collected eggs from the straw, talking all the time about politics, mart prices, space exploration. Melt it down!

Counted new-born lambs trailing umbilical red ribbons. Welcome life! Melt down this shadow in my head!

Had boiled eggs, shop bread and tea—like flame, like water burning, flowing through this image, this past perfect world stamped inside my head.

Standing up suddenly. I had it. I *had* it ...

'Thank you! That was lovely! Goodbye!' I quick-stepped out the door into the dark. Off my rocker, yet smart enough to stop as usual and listen. Awed silence. Then—

'Is he in his right mind?' my uncle slowly enquired.

'I thought he was a Jehovah Witness.'

Laughter.

'And did you get the smell of drink off him?'

'Oh the apple doesn't fall far from the tree.'

'Did ye bring in the yeowes?' My uncle's slow voice turned conversation back to business.

Walking, hitching—Galway to Mayo to Roscommon town—a moth when the candle's out, a bee circling the dead flower; reading the paperback in my pocket, the most crucial book ever written—

'Just as sound is a vibration of sound/silence, the whole universe (that is, existence) is a vibration of solid space ...'

Roscommon to Leitrim and then up to Cavan, blundering, buzzing; eating in pubs, sleeping anywhere, scribbling everything in notebook—

'About forty, she leaned on my shoulder in the kitchen,

whispered—I bet you won't … I crept in after midnight. Cattle bawling outside her window. She was naked … Afterwards she hugged me, then said 'Off you go, go away now, I want to sleep now …'

Cavan to Meath, copying crucial passages of crucial book in crucial notebook—

'For solids and space go together as inseperably as insides and outsides. Space is the relationship between bodies, and without it there can be neither energy nor motion.'

Meath to Dublin, digging my heels in yet moving forwards. Stopping even as I walked to my house to scribble final, stunning insights—

'Now. All has been gathered up. Bring it to a point. *Now.*'

I opened the door. Cat piss stink. Post on mat. *Miaou.* The Siamese cat flickered down the stairs, rubbed against my legs as I picked up the letters.

A stiff cream invitation to the Gonzaga Old Boys' dinner.

A swift written note—I glanced down my father's lines, the advice under-ruled in red.

A postcard photo—Rodin's sculpted hand emerging from a lump of unworked marble—'Love, Ruth.'

Now … I laid them on the table, three cards of divination— past, present, future. Now they must meet.

Past … present … future. Priest … peasant … father. I walked up Palmerston Road, words flying about in my head, steel heeltips sparking on the path, bits of books on my lips—He saith among the trumpets Ha, ha; and he smelleth the battle afar off, the thunder of the captains and the shouting …

No enemy in sight. A sixty-seven-year-old man armchaired alone by the sitting-room fire, head sunk into the suede shoulders of a coffee-coloured cardigan. Not turning as I entered.

'I got your note.'

'That's alright.' Half-looking up.

'How are you?' I stood on the hearth bricks looking down at him. He was weary, dazed as Jamie.

'I don't know what's wrong with me.' On his lap under folded hands—a paperback. Norman Vincent Peale. He raised a hand—*The Power of*—'I just can't seem to …' He put down his hand again.

'Are you not well?'

'I'm fine. I've just been down to Doctor Doyle. He sent me to this—kkmm!—psychiatrist. He said I'm just … depressed.'

'Are you?'

'Ahh. Nothing seems to hold my interest now. I couldn't care if I never held a golf stick.'

'But that happens.'

'It never happened to me. I suppose I hadn't the time to be depressed.'

'Are you still going to work?'

'I put in a few hours every morning. But what's the point? Kevin runs the business now. I'm—kkmm!—redundant.'

'How's Noel?'

'Down on Lough Carra …' He raised the other sallow hand—*Positive Thinking*—made an effort. 'How're you getting on?'

Let's see … Last week I slept with a Cavan farmer's widow. There was an eighteen-year-old actress too. Then there's the gay disco. Oh, and I'm seeing a—kkm!—psychiatrist who thinks I should be in a mental hospital. 'OK,' I said.

'How's the house? Gas little place.'

'Isn't it.' I sat down.

'You all wanted to leave home. We *had* to. I never wanted to—'

He stopped as a car door slammed outside. There was a rattle of stiletto heels on the steps, a click of key in lock. Celia let herself in, sailed into the sitting-room on a wave of perfume.

'I bought you a little present.' She gave my father a pot of Dundee marmalade. 'How are you?'

'That looks nice.'

'I just saw it in Brown Thomas.'

'You must write a lot of cheques.' I hid behind a laugh.

'I don't have a chequebook. If I did, Kennys would be bankrupt!' Celia laughed openly. 'I'm meeting someone for lunch ...' She sailed out again.

And in that moment, as my father drew up his knees slowly and rested the marmalade present on Norman Vincent Peale's book, I saw that power had been transferred; and as happens sometimes in such clear instants, a vista opened—straight as Palmerston Road down which Celia was driving now, down which I could see the future. Sitting opposite my father by the fire, I stretched out my legs, and thought of Percy's Irish proverb—

'The father sits in his son's house
With his knees up under his chin.
The son sits in his father's house
With his feet stretched across the hearth.'

'It's about *power*,' Percy had said.

Power as gentle and persistent as spring water. My mad behaviour which had buffeted my father—that was power. My brother Noel's calm refusal to take his father's place—that was power. Brian's turning his back on power—that was power. And Kevin's marriage to Celia—that was power. It had all happened as naturally as spring water rising from the earth, up through a thousand pores in the limestone. Down the channel now the water would flow, as it snaked down the cressy ditch from Margaret's well, that ditch running into Ganley's meadow and becoming a stream, forcing its way through scraws, breaking them, wearing them loose where they got in the way, tumbling them aside and pouring down to the Dalgan River, which flowed by my mother's old home and in turn became the mighty Clare that drained half Connaught, and finally as the Corrib roared foaming out of Galway city down into the Atlantic.

'If I could only have …' my father fumbled for Norman Vincent Peale words '… been able to *communicate*.'

'Communicate what?'

Long-heavy fingers steadying the jar of Dundee marmalade. 'Maybe I aimed too high—'

'Don't say that.' As I said it I felt something end.

He looked at the clock. 'Will you excuse me for twenty minutes. I have to do my TM.'

'What?'

'Transcendental Meditation. They give you a—kkmm!—mantra.'

Marmalade in one hand, Peale in the other, he walked slowly up to his bedroom.

I walked up to mine. The past. The dark grey suit was hanging in the wardrobe, white shirt in laundry cellophane, tie coiled alongside. While my father lay on his back, I dressed to the nines.

'*Well* …' TM peace or my appearance brought a smile into his face. 'Are you pushing the boat out?'

'I thought I'd go to the school reunion.'

'Why not.'

First, a drink.

The Castle was full of new faces. Through chinks in the crowd I glimpsed the old: Percy, Colin, Jack; Stephen drinking in the corner with a new girl. I pushed to the counter.

'Jamie.'

Jamie resting chin on hand, elbow in a drift of cigarette ash. 'What'll you have?'

'I can't stay.'

'Where are you off to?'

'The University Club.'

'What's that?'

'Jamie, you're great.'

'I know.' Glow.

I blew on it instinctively. 'Will you be here later?'

'Where else would I be?' He resumed gazing through eyes half-shut at the new faces, the river of life.

I walked to the University Club, now incorporating the Kildare Street Club, where once long ago Major Daly had taken me to lunch. That was life too, the middle class now incorporating the Ascendancy class. It was as natural as my sister loving Rich or as Kevin loving Celia. Force, life, power.

'A few coppers.'

A whispery voice from a man, hand out, sitting on legs folded beneath him at the foot of the club's front steps. I recognised him. He had been at school with me.

'Jack?'

A boy like any other boy in school. Becoming gently eccentric then—changing his name to the Irish form, writing only in green ink. Eccentricity hardening or turning to something stronger, stranger. I had seen him next driving an ass and cart down Rathmines Road; then standing outside the Post Office begging. Crowning his career tonight kneeling outside the tall Georgian windows where his old school friends dined.

Slowly he raised his head and stared, silent as a mirror. I scooted up the steps. Force, life, power. Pushed open a tall mahogany door into a drawing-room. A wall of noise—voices and laughter—loud yet discreet, suggesting laughter in court at the judge's joke. How natural this respectability—the climb so long, this place so hard won. So near the surface still the fear of seeming vulgar, but how smothering already the air of satisfaction.

Gorman was home at last, a lecturer in history.

Browne was explaining why he had given up photography and was following his father's footsteps to the Bar. 'My brain was beginning to rot ...'

O'Hara, loosened by a few drinks, suddenly scratched the top of his head, mimed a Haw-Haw laugh—a split-second caricature of our old rector. The O'Conor Don entered, his massive bald red bone head shining like a coronet under the chandelier.

'Everyone is exactly the same.' O'Hara looked around the room, his voice returning to its usual tone, medium dry.

I had another drink.

'Ah, Adrian ...' A voice as soft as Jack's. I turned to Fr Treston, felt a rush of irritation at his mild face, clawed like a climber on smooth cliff-face.

'... And what are you doing these days?'

'Writing, Father.'

'Ah yes—'

'A novel. I've been trying to write a novel for the past five years.'

'Ah—' Fr Treston smile-frowned.

'I gave it up.'

'I suppose that happens.' Smile-frown deepening.

'It wasn't a novel at all.'

'Maybe—'

No, it was nothing, Father. I spent five years writing nothing. Do you know why, Father? So I wouldn't lose anything. What ideal completeness we had in that school of ours, a Renaissance city-state in the suburbs; wrapping our cocks in cotton wool and learning about Dionysus, reading the *Odyssey* and queuing on our knees for Confession. 'I haven't seen you for a long while, Father,' I said.

'No, I've been away, Adrian.'

'I didn't know that, Father.'

'Yes, I've been in mmm Zambia, Adrian, for the past few years.' Fr Treston wound white hands one about the other.

'How did you find it, Father?'

'Full of life, Adrian.' He dipped into a pocket of his light weave jacket, drew out a packet of Camels. 'Full of life.'

'Fr Treston!'

'Ah, Paul ...' And with the same smile-frown, he turned to greet a crimson-faced, ripe-vowelled, well-bellied barrister.

I looked at this priest who saw Aphrodite and Bacchus made flesh in Christ, Aaron's budding rod in the Cross, for whom the magic serpents and sacred groves were contained within the Church. And then he had slipped off to mmm Zambia, which was full of life, the slippery wise Jesuit.

'That was quick.' Jamie's words trembled ash from his cigarette onto his florid tie. He wiped it into a grey smear.

'Not really. It's closing time.'

'Is it?' Jamie raised chin from hand, looked around. 'Where's that girl you were seeing?'

'Kathleen? I don't—'

'No ...' Half asleep, but half awake. 'The other one.'

'Ruth. I'm not seeing her either.'

'You should have asked her to that dinner.'

'I told you, it was an old boys' dinner. Jamie, are you sure you're alright?'

'Will we have a look in Rice's?'

'Let's.' Blow.

Glow.

Fade—going into Rice's. Glow—looking about. But—glow, fade, glow, fade, year after year—the fire was burning low now.

'No luck tonight, Joseph?' He came to rest at the counter next to a swarthy man in a silky navy suit.

'I'm weary of those … boys.'

'Do you know Adrian?' Glow.

'Have I seen you in my gallery?'

'Around the corner?'

'Yes, that's my prison.'

Jamie smiled. 'Joseph's the unhappiest man in Ireland.'

Someone at Jamie's elbow laughed. Jamie in doctor's voice introduced—'Ciarán.'

Ciarán—petty crook with a great thirst—shoved an empty glass into view.

'Come back to my place,' Joseph smiled. 'For a nightcap.'

This was something—this smiling through. This was Stephen with a new girl, Fr Treston smoking Camels in the bush, my father meditating as the family business came down.

We pushed into a wind that met us around South King Street corner. Past the College of Surgeons, under Aesculapius still leaning on his serpent-wreathed club. I thought again of that school where I had spent a decade, where Hebrew and Hellene had scrummed down together; Jesus H. Christ heeling the ball back to Aristotle, who sent it out to I. Loyola, lame in one leg but he had style—selling a dummy to the left, body-swerving to the right and passing it to … me.

'Here we are,' Joseph turned the key, smiled at me.

Jamie stood gazing at the brick wall, gaze tilting upwards looking at the stars? the clouds? 'What was that for?' He pointed to an oval niche high in the façade.

'A head, I believe,' Joseph pushed open the door.

'A head …?' Jamie resumed walking suddenly along the Green, step quickening, skipping in the air and slamming a hand on the STOP sign at Cuffe Street corner. A gong note from the top of the mountain, the end of the line. Then, head down into the breeze, he swung right, disappeared as if into the future: the hospital spell straight ahead, longer than expected; then home to his mother and withdrawal to a suburban routine—walk to the shop for the morning paper, walk again for

the evening paper; his pleasure, his trouble—sex and drink—
banned by his doctor, or by Doctor Jamie himself; giving up
cigarettes almost in boredom; winding down. Most wind down
slowly. Jamie was going out with a bang, bold as that blow on
the STOP sign.

My Virgil gone, his task done. On my own now. Joseph
smiled at me again, I smiled back. So here was where I should
say goodbye to … all my fathers.

We entered a spotless hall of pale varnished floorboards.
Pictures framed in the same pale wood hung along a stairs up to
a kitchen of the same tight good taste. Grey glass table, octagonal white china cups in octagonal black saucers. Joseph made
coffee, thinned by whiskey. Soon we were drinking the
whiskey. 'Drink up.' He sat down, rested a hand on my knee,
then on my thigh.

'How about a bit of music,' Ciarán said.

Joseph went into the next room and Ciarán paused in pouring more whiskey to warn me—Dublin accent smeared with
Oxford—'I can't stand that sort of messing.'

'Goodnight Vienna' came crooning from a record player, followed by Joseph doing a Jack Buchanan glide back to my side.

Ciarán drank more quickly, emptied his cup, looked at the
empty bottle, then at me in confusion or sadness.

Go away—my eyes wished him, as Stephen's eyes had so
often wished me.

'Goodnight.' He got up.

'Goodnight Vienna …' Joseph crooned.

'Very good.' Ciarán laughed, looked away. Joseph was
stroking between my thighs.

'… Where moonlight fills the air with mystery … Just give
the front door a good pull.'

I was drunk, I realized as the slam reached me like a cotton
wool thud. I went into the bathroom—spotless white with a
framed photo of a spotless white bathroom on the wall—and
got sick. Drunk, but sober enough to smile as Joseph called—

'You'll feel better with your trousers off.'

Through the bedroom door I saw him undressing, stubbing out a cigarette in a turquoise glass ashtray.

From the corner of my eye I saw a cigarette smoking in the turquoise glass ashtray, shut my eyes again as I realised someone was sitting astride me. I remembered. Joseph. It was morning. I remembered last night. No hangover. I felt something brush my cheek and, opening my eyes again, saw a silver medallion swing past. Joseph was leaning forward—to kiss me, I thought; in fact to take a deep draw on his cigarette; sitting upright again, riding me. I felt a half-erect cock moving between my thighs. I opened my eyes fully, looked up. But Joseph was looking straight ahead—at a picture maybe. The walls were hung with paintings, individual swirls in identical pale-yellow wood frames. Above the end of the bed hung a cool still life—a red rosehead afloat in a china blue basin of water. Through the doorway I saw others in a line down the pale wood stairs I had ascended last night.

'Morning.' Joseph smiled down at me, then returned to his exercise. That was what it felt like—a morning trot. I looked at him, face brassy anonymous as a mask, his chest lean hard in the slightly unpleasant way of middle-aged fit bodies.

'Well,' he said, 'anything happening?'

Nothing was. I was shrinking from this lest I liked it, afraid to ask the question lest the answer be the wrong one.

Courage—

Slowly my cock raised its head, up out through the warm safe dangerous nest my mother had made, in which the family business had grown; my cock growing, hardening, stiffening; the mud, moss, twigs breaking.

The falling pieces appeared as photos from our mantelpiece battlements. Grandmother: face like a red Indian's, hands—like claws from scrabbling in poor Mayo earth—gathered about half-a-dozen of her children, amongst them my father, barefoot, eyes averted as if from the years ahead. From the next photo: an apprentice boy in Castlerea, Adonis in a thirty-shilling suit, fingers already black from nicotine, no hint of the drink. That showed in the next photo—six inches away, fifteen years later: off the drink now, married, good looks battered, a face like a Mafia man out for revenge as he strides across Capel Street Bridge to business.

'Feels good?' Joseph smiled.

'Yes.' I reached to stroke his cock but he said fussily—

'No, don't do that.' He set to work more earnestly.

I lay back again. I liked the feel of being passive, of feeling Joseph's cock grow between my thighs. I imagined I could get to like it, and many things like it, a lot more some other time with someone else more attractive, younger, less fussy-professional than Joseph. But only as a physical pleasure. I could imagine no romance in this. My emotion would be as detached from what I was doing as that turquoise glass ashtray was from my head. Because that was how I had been formed, conditioned? Maybe. But I had more than enough emotion for women. I wanted suddenly to be doing this with ... I thought of Ruth.

Afterwards, I kissed Joseph's slack snake-bronze cock—at long last I kissed the rod.

'Well?' Joseph said.

'I don't think it's ... me.' That word at last. Me.

'No, I'm afraid you're ...' Joseph smothered a yawn as he swung bony black-haired legs out of bed, put on a white towel dressing-gown '... perfectly normal.'

'I was afraid I might be ... repressed.' I made small-talk of a decade's obsession as I dressed.

'We're all repressed in some way.' He made coffee.

'What way are you?'

'I'm a repressed mediocrity.'

I smiled. 'How about Jamie?'

'Jamie's a repressed saint.'

How good life was! I seemed to feel naked, felt the early morning wind on my skin as I walked down the street scanning faces. From what beds had they come? From what adventures?

Utterly confused and utterly clear, utterly brave and utterly cowardly, I bought a bunch of flowers, and with amber chrysanthemums in their pungent green leaves sprouting from my hand I walked down to Percy Place, to the house next door to where I had been born, where Ruth lived now—

A repressed saint ... A suppressed rant ...

—the dialogue in my head unwinding, sinking to a whisper ... and then silence. The living novel was dead. I was going to live instead. I knocked on the door of the present.

– 14 –

Dickens was right—there are types, not individuals; an infinite number maybe, but each marked by a stamp we have seen somewhere before: the shy hard boy, the beautiful girl with sad eyes—and the young man who has never quite got used to his actions producing results.

You said, 'Will you marry me?'—and the next thing you were in a chapel saying 'I do.'

You invited your friends to a wedding breakfast in the zoo—but still were as surprised to see them there as to see peacocks and monkeys look in the restaurant window.

You booked tickets on the ferry to France—and the next day you were in Paris.

You said, 'Excusez-moi—rue Gay Lussac?'

A polite unsmiling Parisian said, 'Tout droit, monsieur.'

And you were in the Hôtel de l'Avenir, saying, 'Ma femme et moi …'

That was how everything was done. You just did it. And then it was done. It was so simple, it made me afraid, the realization that there is a nerve connecting will and action. It was bearing in on me like water hiccoughing down an air-blocked pipe.

You took a train to Rome—and next day you were lying on your back on the cobblestones of St Peter's Square looking at fountain spray blown sideways by a warm breeze.

You took the train again—and a few nights later you were on the ferry back to Ireland, looking at sea-spray drift over the rails. You do a thing—

'Will we sleep out on the deck?'

'Why not? It's a warm night.'

—the thing is done.

I turned on my side, tucked in behind Ruth, her warm bottom dissolving my stomach knots, and looked across her shoulder at another couple lying out on deck. The young man was asleep. I looked at his face—his lips tight in the middle in doggedness, corners turned up somehow in a light smile. I moved my lips, felt how naturally they moved in a different shape. I lowered my eyebrows as his were lowered, and felt my eyebrows rise again like a bent branch springing back to its own shape.

Ruth murmured something, turned in her sleep, and I lay on my back again. It was dark, the stars familiar from home were sparkling far above the unfamiliar sea. So far. Yet there were stars beyond those stars. I tilted my chin, pursed my lips; they relaxed again into their own shape, and I felt the same intense delight I felt in thinking of the stars going on for ever. I had been loved by my mother, my father—and now I was loved by Ruth: I was as sure of that as I was sure that space went on for ever. Say that was what love was—light by which you could see? The only light by which you could see. Without love you could not imagine infinity.

'I can hear you thinking.' Ruth turned on her side again, and I turned on my side again; now she pressed her stomach to my bottom and we fell asleep.

The big square ship shoved through the waves, the waves closed over again, as they would close over the family business.

You do a thing, the thing is done.

— 15 —

The big evening began badly.

The phone rang, I answered.

'Hello, dear.' My aunt Mae, her voice slightly slurred like a cat's purr. 'Are you all enjoying yourselves?'

'Hello, Mae—'

My mother sent up a hand signal.

'—How do you mean?'

'Oh, the innocent boy.' Claw points showing through the velvet. 'Tell me—in all innocence of course—are you having a little party there?'

'Well, just for the family.'

My mother groaned so deeply that I turned. She was sinking onto the couch, like the Dying Gaul.

'And could you just tell me one other thing.' Mae's voice slipped for a moment into a Mayo accent. She sobbed, got back on track. 'Adrian, could you tell me—what is a religious person?'

'Someone who prays and—'

'And has it got nothing to do with your actions?'

'I suppose—'

'You see, I rang Margaret just now, my own sister Margaret, and she told me you were having an engagement party for Phil.'

'But it's just for Rich's parents—'

'And yet when I rang your mother this morning and asked her was she having an engagement party, she said—quite clearly, quite distinctly—No.'

'But it's not a party, Mae. It's just the family—'

'Oh the little laugh. The snigger. Well, may I say something, dear—when you've finished sniggering.' Sob. Then a hiccough. She was drunk. 'We mightn't all have the grand accent and the big house up in Cowper Road, but certain people were glad enough to have us when they first came to this town—'

'Ah, Mae, don't be mad—'

'There's far madder on your mother's side, dear. There's your uncle Paul for a start …' Sob. 'And your father. I found him in the gutter. He was a drunken bum. B.U.M.—Bum. But I took him out of the gutter, because he was my brother, my own family.' Sob.

'Do you want to talk to him?'

'No, dear. I don't want to talk to him. Not for as long as I live, and that won't be long.' Now she was crying. 'Maybe we hadn't a great education, no more than anyone then, but at least we—'

'Mae, I'll have to go.'

'Oh the maneen has to go. Go on.' Her voice recovered. 'Could you tell me before you go what the menu is tonight? Salmon? Lobster? Oh, sorry, am I interrupting the little laugh again? Ah yes, I hear the little laugh. Or is it more of a titter, would you say? Yes, I think it's more of a little girl's titter.' Sob. 'Isn't that a nice word—titter? But of course you'd know that already, wouldn't you, being a writer.'

'Goodbye, Mae.'

'Goodbye, Miss Titter.'

My mother rose again. She had two tones of voice: the one she used for ordinary life, for everything from death to ecstasy; and this one, used when her family was involved—something between a groan and a hiss. *Why did you tell her?*

'Why didn't you?'

'I'm not able for this.' Massaging his heart gently, my father walked out to the conservatory. He addressed the flowers. 'I'm just not able for this ...'

'Jesus,' she rested a hand on the amber table-top, 'if you upset Dada.'

He continued walking, out into the back garden. She went back into the kitchen.

The tension remained in the air, heavy as the scent of cooking, yet my mother moved calmly through it. Her face appeared now and then at the service-hatch showing anxiety, pleasure—and something wilder, brighter. Looking at her, I realized that in a way this evening was the climax of her life. Her only daughter was to marry, Rich was coming to supper with his parents: that was the anxiety and the pleasure. The wilder, brighter glow was kindled by Rich's past. His family had been landed gentry. The face disappeared, reappeared hot from the stove.

Glimpsing her almost savage glow, I was reminded of a day I had been driving her through autumn countryside, when we met a fox hunt, and I had stopped to let it go by; and there, in the clatter of horseshoes on roadmetal, the slap of falling dung, the howl-music of horn and hounds, the opera-loud colours and voices, I had seen my mother's glowing awe. That world was her reality still, I had realized as she spent the rest of the journey talking about the East Galway of her childhood; describing the Misses This dressing the altar, Major That walking to the front seat at Sunday Mass.

Much more to it than that of course. Rich was a nice boy, with a job; his father was landless now, but his grandfather might once have been landlord of my mother's family—for Mr Coote's family had also come from the West of Ireland. It was that connection which fired the wildest glow in the aureole about my mother's face: the peasants of centuries past were at last drawn abreast of their old masters. The family business had succeeded.

'Would you ever go out to the garden'—her head appeared at the hatch again, looking in at the dining-room clock, interrupting my thoughts—'and cut some roses for the table.'

My father was strolling about, nipping off blown flowers, wiping greenfly-smeared nails clean; taking up a putter leaning against the wash-house wall and tapping a ball across the lawn; fidgety but content. For he too, like all decent peasants, was a snob. His daughter was to be married, and to a Good Family. He had led his tribe through the desert. The brutal forty-year shove uphill was over. From the summit he looked down upon the promised land.

Sww-ing sw-issh! He swung the putter as a driver, sending daisy heads flying. I moved about the garden with the scissors, snipping blooms. Above the apple trees—the back of Jamie's house, his bedroom curtains still closed.

'What time are they coming?'

'Seven.' My father held out a hand—that habit of power still with him. I handed him the scissors and he snipped a sucker from a standard rose tree. 'No sign of Noel?'

Silence, dripping with vinegar and honey.

'How is he?' Wanting suddenly to be close to, intimate with my father, I handed my brother over for a roasting.

Got back instead the protective father's gaze. 'Noel doesn't lose any sleep over the business—and bloody good luck to him. I only wish I could be like him.' He looked up at a wavery V of seagulls drifting down the evening sky towards Sandymount; added, as if thinking aloud alone—'I always hated it myself. Kkmm! But it was the only thing I could do.'

Winded, as if punched in the stomach, I stared, and waited for my father to continue, but the only sound was the dog suddenly yapping.

'That'll be them.' He leaned the putter against the wall and went inside, drawing a clinging fold of trouser cloth from his buttock cleft.

One thing was wanting now: that Rich's parents be as nervous as Rich had said they were. And they were. My mother's cup overflowed. Nerves, illness, Harry Morton's wooden leg she could manage, indeed were meat and drink to her. It was confidence, so easily becoming condescension, that over-whelmed her. But Mr Coote entered as if through deep snow, his face rigid pale—mirroring my father's as he toiled across the carpet to shake hands.

The rich Oxford voice was a whisper, the feudal crest cut in a green stone set in a gold ring vanished into a clenched hand, opening only to take a glass of gin and tonic, closing on it in relief. Then little by little, like the tonic bubbles bursting to the surface, conversation began.

Oh sweet air. For all the deep pleasure talking with my father gave me, I felt relieved, a diver back above water, as I breathed in the Cootes' light general conversation, beautiful impersonal chat. More beautiful still was hearing my parents join in.

You can do it!—I wanted to say—You don't have to talk about family and business all the time. In fact you don't have to talk about the family ever again. Oh be like this always. Go on, Dada! Carry on reminiscing about the old Gate Theatre … Aidan Grennell … Iris Lawlor … Lord Longford's big belly and the collection box he held before it. And the old woman who played the harp in Wicklow Street with a big seashell at her feet for pennies. Go on, Dada—have another Lucozade, tell us more about the day you followed Jack Doyle down Grafton Street to admire him. Go on, you closet dandy, describe his woman's waist again, his perfect shoulders. Yes! Yes! Another G and T, Mr Coote. Imitate the mouse in your kitchen again—Ee-ee-eek!

'Not EEC?' My father smiled like a boy.

Dada, I could kiss you. Laugh like that again, Mama! Step out of the family rath. Forget about poor Mae drinking in her flat and weeping about the past. Leave the past. Kevin is married, I'm married, your daughter is getting married. Let's all fly away, each in his own direction, to meet now and then for lovely meaningless chat like this. Join in. Talk about anything, talk about nothing. Ssh! Listen to Mr Coote now going on about London. Mass at the Oratory, then down to buy the old *D.T.* and then into The Grapes to read it over a good G and T—

'That's my idea of heaven.'

'It's not mine,' Mrs Coote said.

'No, it's not yours, darling, is it?'

The spaniel yapped again, the key turned in the door. 'That'll be Kevin and Celia.' My mother stiffened. 'Or Brian ...' She glanced out her porthole, the windowpane left free of muslin curtain. 'Oh no, it's Noel ...'

Relax, Mama! Why can't you relax? Class? But you'd be the same if one of your old country friends was here.

'I'll just let him in ...'

How often her timidity had made me rage, but now, looking at her wary unsure face slip away, I saw how lonely, limited a life she had—envied by, cut off from, the poor country she had left. She might have been accepted by her snobbish neighbours here if it wasn't for her self-consciousness, for which there was no cure, since it sprang from her own snobbery. For she saw these neighbours as 'Johnny jump ups', 'Beggars on horseback', ridiculous imitators of the gentry who alone merited the fear and hate worthy of respect. And now one of those gentry was in her sitting-room.

She vanished with Noel into the kitchen, and I wondered again how someone so at ease on her home ground—here, alone with her family, she would comment with an intelligence that amazed me—how could she be stamped by such pettiness?

But it wasn't pettiness to her. Her mind was like one of those attics dismissed as 'full of junk', but whose every cobwebbed item is known. Compared with her folk-memory, surveys and statistics were crude generalizations. She could have drawn a social map of her native parish accurate to a hundred decimal places; every field, parish priest and snub every family had received over three generations was burnt into her. Here was the triumph of the unread, here too a source of my indecision with words—pale symbols, in my mother's eyes, of reality. Sometimes she sat down to read a book, but dropped it like a stale crust when real nourishment, news of flesh and blood, came to hand.

Here she was at a distance from it all, but that only heightened her vision. And yet she was indifferent to the country as only country people can be. The day we had met the fox hunt, I had been driving her at long last to visit that old country home, listening to her stream of memories grow into a spate as we approached the holy spot; and been amazed more than appalled when she lost her way in the last few miles. We drove past her house without her recognizing it. She was like an artist, I thought, whose image of the past had replaced the past.

If she had stayed or emigrated, the place's reality or a job in Leeds or New Jersey would have scoured out a channel, carried that past away. As it was, her cut-off comfortable life so near, so far from that past, had made a dam and the waters formed a lake, the lake I had almost drowned in.

This house was her crannóg in that lake. From here she could sortie, retreat to digest what she had seen and heard; through letters, phone calls she could follow families' risings and fallings.

This was what I had defended myself against since childhood's end. She would never get me into her crannóg. That secret self was what I was discovering now in the turbulent confidence which marriage had brought. I was thirsty for it all the time, as hungry for it as for sex. Even here, now, as Mr Coote threw back the gins and conversation flowed, I slipped away from them, from Ruth my new wife too, to walk the back garden and feast on this self of mine that was daily growing more visible; real as the stone walls and houses that appeared in Blessington Lake when the waters fell. I had burnt my Real Novel, at last found a worthy conclusion for my hero—in flames. Some day I would write *about* him: a poor substitute for a living walking talking novel, but—like my father—it was the only thing I could do ...

As I returned through the dining-room, my mother's head appeared at the service-hatch, glowing—if possible—even more; glowing like her Sacred Heart picture at night when the lamp shone red upon it. Behind her in the kitchen my brother Noel paced smiling, white-faced. Something was up. What was up?

The doorbell rang again—and now my mother's face was incandescent. 'That'll be Eileen,' she hissed. 'He's just told me they're getting married. Don't say a word till dinner. He's going to announce it then.'

Noel went to let in his fiancée, his face deathly pale.

Why?

First, for the obvious reasons. Eldest son Noel had taken it all on the chin; taken in the first dark years as our father stayed off the drink, battled out cold sober each morning to his first shop, returned dazed each evening from another day beating his head on the red brick wall of commerce; Noel already withdrawing instinctively; in his shell by the time he went to school.

'Why are you always hanging out of someone!'—our father's angry/guilty remark as Noel walked home from school arm in arm with or leaning on the shoulder of a bigger boy. 'Can you not walk on your own?'

Our father walking on his own by then, sober, more prosperous, his generosity set free; his children growing up, small trees behind a windbreak. But Noel was already bent inalterably by the wild west wind; Noel was sure of one thing—he wasn't going to follow in his father's footsteps, or any footsteps that lead to a life like his father's.

A closer look now as he returns from the hall with Eileen, lovely Eileen from Mayo, Eileen his mother's and father's Connaught past embodied, Eileen whom he can no more marry than he can return to his mother's womb. Look at him: hair bleached boy-blonde by Lough Carra sun, where he has been fishing with Eileen's father, who has a fishing-tackle shop in Castlebar, a shop as simple as his own father's first shop. Hair as blonde as in that photo on the mantelpiece, first family photo taken—Noel smiling alone between mother and father, in soft focus by Lafayette; focus of hopes, born on Christmas morning, their Christ child. Noel, the family flaw, the straw that binds the bricks, the one in every family who takes it all too seriously, or never took it seriously at all. Noel seeing his brothers, sister growing up and away, marrying, wading ashore from his mother's great lake; Noel trying to sink into those warm waters once more; those waters he hates for he knows they have trapped him; those waters he loves for so long they have protected him. Noel taking the big step now—

'Eileen and I are getting married ...'

There was a moment's silence, a whirling of expressions like the times and places changing on a railway station noticeboard. Then, looking delighted, which made him look like a child, our father breathed—

'Well ...!'

—and smiled across the table into Noel's eyes, eyes he had known for thirty-seven years. Baby-wide eyes avoiding him as—silent menacing demented from another bad day's business—he came into the little kitchen of our house in Kimmage Road West. Boy-blue eyes tense in school photos. Adult eyes peaceful by rivers, loughs as Noel flicked the rod and laid an oiled silk line on the water, line walking on tiptoe, dry fly cocked upright sitting on the skin of the water; effortless perfection.

Eyes seeming easy now, Noel drifted on the digressions, jokes, and toasts his announcement gave rise to. The heat was off. Perhaps the whole thing would go away—as business problems went away when his father or brother appeared.

Brother Kevin's eyes met Celia's glance across the table, glanced away again, but what their eyes said remained in the air like a spark when two flints are struck together in the dark—

If Noel marries Eileen, we're finished.

[215]

Kevin finished, trapped under that giant yellow straw sombrero forever.

Celia finished, trapped in this island off her Mainland.

The prodigal son was feasting on the fatted calf; the son who had toiled obediently at home was being ignored. That; but imagine if in the parable the prodigal son had arrived home with a woman met while he rioted in a far country. And if that woman supported the returned prodigal, insisted on full rights ...

A strange detail remains in my memory of that evening: the Sacred Heart lamp was out. Sometimes the socket was used for an electric fire to heat the room before dinner, but afterwards the lamp was plugged in again, the vestal fire at once rekindled. This evening the plug lay on the floor. Why? In case the Cootes saw this symbol of a peasant hearth? That peasant hearth at last abandoned? Or simply forgotten in the excitement of Noel's announcement? Whatever the reason, whatever about the vase of full-flowered roses on the table, we celebrated under a dead bulb.

But what celebrations! What prodigal musik from Mr Coote after dinner, when he sat on the piano stool, set his glass on the piano top, and began to play. Blues and ragtime flowing out from under those white hands. My father offering then to play his party piece—'A Cigarette with Lipstick Traces'—not heard in years. A trial vamp, then he turned to tell—our father telling to strangers!—a story of his country youth.

Telling of how he had played in a band in Ballyhaunis, how they had gone one night to play in Ballinlough, where he had played this very song; when the parish priest had sprung up onto the stage, stopped them, stopped the dance, and announced— over to our father, speaking not in his bland weather forecaster voice, but in laughing imitation of the priest's Maynooth-machine voice—'If that's the best Ballyhaunis can do, they can go back home again!'

'Sure those priests,' my mother said—Mama speaking in public! Venturing an opinion! What an opinion!—'they had the people brow-beaten ...'

I switched off, returned to my own thoughts. That novel I had toiled at for so many years, those years themselves—what was it, what were they but an attempt to express what this evening's celebration was expressing? Now at last the past was being made present, the country brought to the city, man joined with woman, Anglo joined with Irish, the poor made rich, the inarticulate made articulate, the passive made active, the hidden revealed, water brought to land. As I had hidden in that novel, in the country, the inarticulate, the passive—so had my brother Noel hidden in lakes and streams. As I had used writing, he had used angling. Now he was stepping out from his father's long shadow, from his mother's protective waters, and wading ashore to marry.

Now I was married, was making my way out of that marsh—half novel, half life—onto solid land; at last, life and art, family and business were distinct ...

'A cigarette with lipstick traces
An airline ticket to romantic places ...'

My father was playing, Mr Coote singing, everyone standing, joining in—

'These simple things remind me of you ...'

Celia glanced at Kevin, he followed her glance, I followed both their glances. Noel was drifting away from Eileen's side, sidling out the door.

I returned to my thread of grandiose thought, searched for an image of that submerged world at last being made manifest.

Yes, it was coming to the surface now, pumped up from a great depth, rising through ignorance, failure, fear, timidity—a great ship, sunk for centuries, through whose riggings fish had swum, coming up at last to daylight where—

I heard the creak of the downstairs toilet door, above the singing heard the distinct, horrible, unmistakable sound of retching, then a vomit gush.

—I followed my simile to its end. But up in the daylight the air was too much, and the whole raised galleon—brazen full-bosomed figurehead jutting from the prow, rigging tangled with seaweed, hull sparkling with salt rime—crumbled to nothing.

The phone rang. Again I answered. Aunt Mae again.

    'Whell, dhear …' She was plastered. 'Finished, are ye?'

    'Yes,' I said. 'Finished.'

− The Beginning The End −

Ruth was in The Coombe.
  Percy was in St James's.
  Noel was in St Edmondsbury.
  Jamie was in St Loman's.

I started at The Coombe and worked outwards.

A baby girl.
  'My little seagull.'
  'Why do you call her that?'
  'That was the first thing I heard after she was born.' Ruth looked out the window 'He flew past there, calling.'
  I stroked my daughter's wet spiky little head. Her lips, limpeted to the nipple, sucked milk in ravenous gulps.

An old man.
  Without his toupee, his teeth, Percy was like a skeleton.
  'How are you?'

'I twied …' He smiled, as proud-looking as my wife.

He had swallowed a bottle of aspirins, washed them down with a bottle of dwy shewwy.

'How's life?'

Noel had the calm of the tranquillized.

'I brought you the paper.'

He glanced at the headline—Ninth Anniversary of Intern-ment: Three Killed, Eighteen Injured—and handed it back. 'We get it here.'

'And this month's *Salmon and Trout*.'

He flicked through the magazine. 'God—old Balfour-Kinnear is still going.'

'What's it like here?'

'Alright.'

'Do you need anything?'

Calm tranquillized, but still the dry smile; not an imitation of our father's but his own, the real thing now. 'The Liffey's at the bottom of the garden. You could bring me out one of my rods.'

'Will we have a look?'

Anything to get out of this brown luxury hotel for the wretched. We walked down a gravel path by banks of stinking wild garlic to where Anna Livia flowed.

'Seriously, why don't I bring you a rod? Which would you like—the Hardy?'

'It's OK. I'll be out next week.'

'What will you do?'

That smile again.

I made conversation. 'Many visitors?'

'Kevin and Celia dropped in for a chat.' Still smiling.

I looked at the river flowing past, nudging a stick, loosening a scraw, a bottle wedged in the bank; carrying sticks, scraws, bottles before it. That was how it would be, that was how the family business would go.

Conversation slipping, we walked back up the slope to the house. A thrush was delivering the full spring song.

'And Eileen was out to see me.'

'How is she?'

'She looked into my house, to see everything was alright.'

'Good.'

'I was burgled.'

'Oh no. Anything taken?'

That dry smile again. 'The engagement ring.'

'Jamie.'

Another doped smile. 'You're very good to come out. Everyone's very good.'

'Many visitors?'

'Stephen's just gone.'

'He got married.'

'So he said. She's an artist.'

'And Helen married Denis.'

'Everyone's married.'

'Except Barrett.'

'They parted?'

'He's back in town.'

Jamie nodded slowly. 'Well done.'

I sat in a plastic chair by his bed. 'How are you?'

'You couldn't just reach over to the locker—'

A green litre of Seven-Up in a bower of Get Well cards, a pack of felt-tip markers ...

'For what?'

'There's an exercise book—'

'This?'

'Yeh.' He opened it, vaguely, at random, handed it to me. The page was decorated about the margins with zig-zags, chevrons of blue, pink, green. In the middle—a poem:

The sun in the east
The moon in the west
Such joy in my breast.

'What do you think?'
'That's beautiful, Jamie.'
'You like that one?'
'Yes. I do.'
He tore out the page and handed it to me.